Financial Statements

The Ultimate Guide to Financial Statement Analysis for Business Owners and Investors

Contents

Introduction

Imagine a press release on your desk. "General Consolidated increases revenues by 90%," it says. That has to be good news. Should you rush out to buy the shares?

Let's look a little further down the press release. General Consolidated didn't tell you in the top line what had happened to profits: they're flat.

Now you might just think, okay, profits are flat. But think about what the relationship between the two numbers means; General Consolidated has obviously had a huge squeeze on margins. Put simply, it made a heck of a lot more profit on each dollar of sales last year than it did this year. Does that still sound like a company you'd want to own shares in?

This book aims to teach you how to read financial statements in this way, looking behind the figures on the page to see how the real business is doing. In some ways it's a bit like being a detective; something happened, and you're depending on footprints, fingerprints and affidavits to try to work out exactly what went on. You'll need to do a bit of reading between the lines, and you'll also want to try to link what you see happening in the numbers with what you see in the 'real' world. For instance, if every General Consolidated store you drive past has a fire sale going on, you know why profit margins have taken a dive!

If you have your own business, understanding financial statements better will help you get more profit out of your business, and this will also help you recognize warning signs in the accounts. Too many business owners run their companies on the basis of month-on-month sales comparisons. Knowing your way around financial statements will help you spot trends in working capital that might mean you need to raise fresh finance, for example. You'll also be able to use financial statements of other companies in your sector to set your business benchmarks that can help improve your performance.

This book starts with a little introduction to accounting basics - the principles behind financial statements - and to the auditing process, just to set the scene. Then we go through the three main statements - profit and loss, balance sheet, and cash flow - and explain how they work and what the different items in them mean. After that, we get into the real meat of the book, looking at sample accounts and discussing how to calculate ratios that will tell you a lot about the health of the business. Also, where to look in the notes to the accounts to find out 'where the bodies are buried'!

We'd also encourage you to try out your newly acquired skills on other publicly available financial statements. Why not start with a couple of companies you have shares in or a couple of businesses in your own sector?

This is not a book for auditors. We won't teach you the abstruse requirements of detailed subclauses in the statements of generally accepted accounting principles (GAAP). We'll talk about a few contentious accounting practices, but the aim is to help you understand how companies can polish up lackluster results, and where to look to find out if they've done so.

If you need an auditor, whether to produce your own business's accounts or to look into the accounts of a business you're thinking of buying, you'll need to get a professional. But having read this book, you'll have a better idea of what your auditor needs to know, what questions you might want to ask, and what the figures actually mean once your auditor has produced them.

Throughout this book, we're going to use two real sets of accounts to look at, so that you're used to using financial statements in the real world, and to make sure that what you're learning reflects the difficulties and ambiguities of real accounts rather than nicely planned textbook examples. Sometimes we're going to take shortcuts that a chartered financial analyst would tell you are a bit doubtful - to save time or to simplify, and also because, if you're looking at financial statements for your own purposes, it's more important to understand why you might include or exclude a given item than to use a formula 'correctly.' While auditors like right answers, looking at financial statements is more about asking the right questions.

The two sets of accounts we'll use are from retailer Sears, and airplane manufacturer Airbus. One is based in the US, the other in the Netherlands, so they use slightly different accounting principles as well as different currencies, but you'll see that they use exactly the same basic accounting concepts and differ only in the details. They're two very different kinds of business and that's why we selected them, because the ratios that are important to one business are different from the ratios that matter to the other. Also because you'll see that the ratios applicable to businesses vary very greatly from industry to industry.

Chapter 1 – Accounts and Audit

<u>Basic principles of accounting</u>

Let's kick off with what accountants learn in the very first lesson they take: the twelve basic principles of accounting. Some are quite simple while others are more complex, but you can't make up a set of accounts without understanding them. They are, so to speak, the different keys and chords you can use to write a song, or the basic grammar you need to write a sentence.

1. The accounting entity. The business is separate from its owners (even if some small business bosses behave as if this wasn't the case); it is a free-standing, distinct entity. Among other things, this means that if you own a business and you occasionally borrow from the petty cash, or put your own money into the business, you need to issue an IOU or give yourself shares or a loan note. It also means that even if a company is controlled by a larger company, it still needs to produce its own accounts.

2. Going concern - the business producing financial statements needs to be operating, and expected to continue to do so. If it's insolvent, or it's on the verge of going bankrupt, or there are severe doubts about whether it can refinance, the auditors have to add a *going concern qualification* to the accounts. This is a warning to investors and creditors that the company may not be around much longer. A going concern

qualification doesn't mean that the company *will* fail, but it means there are real doubts about its ability to continue.

3. Measurement is vital. If a thing can't be measured, and measured in monetary terms, it can't go in the financial statements. Customer satisfaction is important; product design and quality is important; innovation is important. But none of these can be objectively measured, or measured in purely financial terms, so they can't go in the financial statements (they can, and often do, go in the management report on operations).

4. Units of measurement. You need a standard unit of measurement. In the US, that would be dollars; elsewhere, pounds, euros, yen, baht, lari or ngultrum. You may, of course, be of a size to produce your accounts in millions of dollars - in which case a simple note at the head of each column suffices.

5. Historical cost. Accounting is about history. It's not about making forecasts. Nor is it about what things are worth today. Take a machine that you bought ten years ago for $1,000. It might, today, be worth $2,000, if it's old and rare and specialized, or nothing, if it's obsolete. The accounts say it's worth what you paid for it (less depreciation, but we'll talk about that a bit later). Everything in the accounts goes in at historical cost. Imagine we look at your house or apartment - we take the price you paid for it, whatever's happened to real estate in your neighborhood since then, and we add the price you actually paid for everything in the house - and we say that's your net worth. And since you decorated yourself, the décor is worth exactly what you paid for the paint, even if you're an ace interior designer with your own home staging business. Well, a financial advisor might not be too impressed by that - but it's the way financial statements work out the net worth of a business.

6. Materiality. "It's not material," accountants sometimes say. When an item is very small, and wouldn't change the overall figures by much, it's not material. It's very much the auditor's judgment call as to whether an item is material or not, based on whether the auditor thinks a reasonable person's judgment relying on the information would be changed or influenced by relying on the misstatement, or omission. Many people use a rough rule of thumb of 5% of total when working out whether a figure is material, but that's not sacrosanct.

7. Estimates and judgments might seem opposed to the certainty of the historical cost basis, but in fact they are quite frequently included in financial statements. For instance, some liabilities are shown at a carrying amount that includes an estimate of future obligations associated with it. The important thing is that such estimates are made methodically and consistently, and their basis disclosed.

8. Consistency is at the heart of financial statements. You don't choose one way of doing things one year, then adopt another way of doing them the year after. You don't chop and change. That also means you need to keep records of accounting policies, so that you're sure you always apply the same rules. It also means that if one part of your business uses a particular type of accounting, all your businesses should probably do it that way (though when we look at the Sears accounts in detail we'll see that Sears and Kmart account for inventories in two different ways. Presumably changing Kmart over to the Sears accounting method just didn't cost in.)

9. Conservatism. No, this isn't about politics - it's about always giving the most conservative view of a business's financial statements, tending to give a lower figure for revenues, and higher figures for costs. Auditors are not the kind of people who'd be happy in advertising or marketing roles - their job is about giving the most downbeat appreciation of prospects,

not about trying to 'sell' the financial figures. For instance, although inventory is normally valued at historical cost (principle 5, which we already talked about), if it's old and perhaps obsolete, like a load of stock of four-year-old smartphone models, then conservatism says you should value it at the *lower* of historic cost and actual value. If you bought the phones at $180 each but now they're only selling for $150 on ebay, you need to write off $30 on the value of each phone to reflect that. Another example would be that of litigation - conservatism says you mustn't anticipate the result of winning a case, but you *must* show the estimated impact of losing it.

10. Periodicity is another basic concept. Your financial statements are made up for a given period, whether that's a week, a month, or - for 99% of public company financial statements - a year. So when you compare two periods, you should be comparing apples with apples - not pears, bananas, or breadfruit. (Only occasionally, companies decide to change their year-ends, or have mergers partway through a year, and you end up with odd periods like fifteen months or nine months.)

11. Substance over form. The financial statements should always represent business reality - the economic reality that we're talking about - and not just the form of transactions. So for instance, you might think you could bump up your revenues by selling yourself a product, selling it back to the company, and bouncing it between the two of you a few times. The statements should 'see through' that transaction - it's not real. Special-purpose vehicles, invoicing before the goods have been supplied, and similar window-dressing techniques *should* be barred according to this principle - though there are always a few that sneak through.

12. Accruals basis. Sums are 'accrued' over a period, that is, they are spread out either according to time (a one-off annual

insurance premium will be accounted for at a rate of one-twelfth for each of the months to which it applies) or matched with the relevant revenues. And revenues are reported when they are earned, not when the customer actually pays. The accruals basis means that the profit and loss account doesn't represent the movement of cash in the business - for that, you'll have to look at the cash flow account. The accruals basis is probably the single part of accounting that most people have a problem with, and we have a whole chapter about depreciation and amortisation later one. Basically, think of it as reflecting the fact that we don't do everything with cash, we don't always pay on the nail, and sometimes we invest for the future and expect to get our money back over a period of time. That's why we need accruals - dealing with the impact of time on our financial statements.

That's quite a lot to be involved with! But it doesn't mean that everything's cut and dried. As we'll see when we talk about depreciation, a lot of things are left up to the judgment of individual accountants, and different treatments of the same accounting data are possible. But these basic principles are always present in any set of financial statements, and although different accountants and companies might use different policies, they should all obey these basic principles. (Imagine an orchestra - the violins have one tune, the cellos another, the flutes are playing up top and the soloist is playing something else entirely, but they're all in three-four waltz time and they're all playing in D major.)

<u>The audit</u>

Although a smaller company may be exempt from needing an audit, most larger businesses are required to have an audit carried out. The audit process involves an independent, qualified accountant, or team of accountants, assessing the company's systems and checking that the financial statements are a true and fair representation of the company's state of affairs.

Understanding financial statements also means understanding the auditing process. An auditor will look at documents to draft an audit plan - those documents might include board minutes, bank statements, receipts, ledgers, organization charts, and process documentation. While most of them are financial documents, auditors are also interested in management decisions and work processes, to enable them to relate the figures to the way the business is operating. So, they may ask for more general documentation to be made available. They will also look at the financial systems of the business and how finance is controlled.

They'll then identify the major risks. For instance, they may find that sales are often badly recorded, perhaps missing out on, or miscalculating discounts that have been given. They may express some concern that only one person in the business has access to the finance software. That's bad practice, as it means no one can check the data for fraud or error. The auditors will generally report to the company, summarizing problems they have found: poor systems or poor controls, errors and discrepancies, and potentially contentious accounting policies.

A plan will then be made for fieldwork, and the audit team will check sample entries in the accounts to check that items have been correctly recorded. The auditors will also look at the accounting policies that have been used in preparing the financial statements. It's quite possible that they will ask the company to change the way it reports some items, to bring it into line with generally accepted principles.

The auditor's report is published with the financial statements. Generally, the auditors give an unqualified report; this means that:

- The financial statements comply with GAAP
- They comply with relevant regulatory requirements
- All material items have been adequately disclosed
- Any changes in accounting policies have been disclosed

An unqualified report relates only to the financial statements; it's not a clean bill of health for the business itself, but simply says the statements are a true and fair representation of the business's finances.

A qualified report might be issued if the accountant can't for some reason audit one area of the statements (e.g., stocks held in a foreign subsidiary), or if there is a single misstatement (a figure that does not comply with GAAP). An explanatory paragraph will be added to the report explaining the issue.

An auditor might also issue an adverse opinion. That's much more serious - it means that the financial statements are materially misstated. It's very unusual for an auditor to issue such a report. Usually, companies will work hard to ensure they provide the information required and that their accounting policies comply with GAAP and with their auditor's views.

An auditor's life

What do auditors actually do? From the top level it all looks very planned and scheduled - at ground level, it's a very 'bitty' job. A junior auditor may be zooming all over an organization for half-hour meetings trying to find out why there's a variance between two sets of figures, or why a client's customer thinks they still owe $20,000 on a receipt but the accounts show $24,000 outstanding. What happened? Is it the audit client's systems that are wrong, or the customer's?

Some people are easy to track down; others, particularly salespeople, can be difficult to get hold of. In an audit of a multinational company, some auditors start early in the morning or stay late into the night to ensure they can get hold of finance staff in foreign subsidiaries in widely different time zones.

Some questions will be solved easily, while others can require several phases of follow-up including getting in touch with customers and suppliers. An auditor could have six or seven meetings in a day, and at the same time will be following up previous meetings via phone calls or emails.

While the auditor is following up the different testing procedures laid down in the audit plan, and questions arising from those tests, it becomes very messy once there's a variance that needs to be reconciled or an issue has been identified. Even finding out who's responsible for a certain item can be tricky - and coaxing a reticent or obstinate member of staff to give out the right information demands people skills at a high level!

Everything has to be documented. Once documented, it has to be analysed - do the answers solve the problem, or do further tests or interviews need to be carried out? It may be that the original plan didn't include extensive tests of, say, accounts receivable, as that system was considered robust - if there are a lot of issues with individual large contracts, that decision might need to be revisited. A junior auditor won't take that decision on his own, but will always refer up to the audit senior - who might want to change the testing approach.

Keeping up with other people in the team is a huge effort. To ensure you're always working on the same documents, you have to keep connected to the same database - you can't run the risk of two sets of figures gradually diverging from each other. Keeping other people posted, giving the senior auditor regular status updates, and making sure you're always in the swim, make life as an auditor much more of a challenge than most people outside the profession realise!

Chapter 2 – The Profit and Loss Account

Profit is what the newspaper stories always lead with. Wall Street is obsessed with quarterly earnings statements. No one ever headlines an article "Oracle strengthens balance sheet" or "Microsoft increases net asset value." It's profit - profit all the way. So naturally, we're going to turn to the profit and loss account first.

The P&L (as it's known for short) is all about subtraction. Start at the top with total revenue, and then subtract costs, in order to arrive, at the bottom, at the net profit. This means the profit after all the costs of operating the business, interest to service its debts, and that regrettable but inevitable obligation: tax.

So that's a pretty easy concept. Let's first take a look at the different costs reported in the P&L, and the different levels of profitability, and what they mean to a business.

- Revenues. Remember that the accruals concept means that revenues are reported when they are earned, so this isn't a cash number. In fact, software companies regularly have a special sales effort to get contracts signed in the last month of the financial year so they can report the revenue. It doesn't matter that the customer won't actually pay up until two or three months down the line. On the other hand, an accountant, architect or lawyer may have worked billable hours during the reporting period and not yet have invoiced them. Remember also to look at the notes to the accounts for the specific policies applied.

- Cost of goods sold. For a retailer or manufacturer, this is crucial. For a hotel, less so. It's the cost of the goods that you sold - they might come out of stock, or you might have bought them in the period. And remember, the accruals basis means that stock you've bought in the period reported, but haven't sold, doesn't count - it's going to be kept on the balance sheet (another example of where the P&L differs from the cash accounts).

- Some companies will show cost of services. For instance, the cost per billable hour is a direct cost of revenue. On the other hand, time spent in marketing activities isn't billable, so a consulting firm needs to be careful about the system for reporting time spent on different activities.

- Gross margin is calculated as revenues less the cost of goods sold. For instance if a retailer buys notebooks at $0.50 each and sells them for $2, the gross margin is 75%. That's 2 - 0.50 = 1.50, which gives us the gross profit, and then 1.50 / 2 % gives us the gross margin. That's a pretty good gross margin, by the way!

- Next come all the indirect costs of the business - the costs that aren't directly related to sales. Premises costs (rent, electricity, insurance, maintenance), selling and marketing costs, and administrative costs, all figure in here. Again, the accruals concept applies, so if you pay your insurance annually and the premium went up halfway through the year, you'll show six months at the old rate and six months at the new higher rate. The rest of your new, higher premium is 'banked' in the balance sheet and you'll use it up next year.

- The next cost is a complete fiction, but an important one, depreciation and amortization. It's really important, so we've given it its own chapter later on, and it's probably the single most important application of the accruals basis for many firms. When you spend money on a capital asset like manufacturing plant or a server farm, you don't take 100% of it as a cost to the P&L that year. Instead, you think about how long the asset will last, and you *amortize* the cost over that period. Applied to my wardrobe, if I buy a pair of jeans for $30 and I think they'll last ten years before I put them in the trash, I'd amortize that cost at $3 a year. So this is a fictional item, in that it's non-cash, but it's actually quite a sensible way of dealing with the fact that businesses often spend amounts disproportionate to their annual income on major assets that are expected to generate income in future.

- There might also be *impairment charges*, which again don't reflect a cash movement, but are the result of taking a fresh look at the value of the business's assets on the balance sheet. Perhaps the company bought a new business and now realizes it overpaid.

- Operating profit or EBIT (earnings before interest and taxes) is what we get when we take these indirect costs out of gross profit. This is the level at which we see what the business would make if it didn't have any debt (or any cash in the bank), so it's a good level for comparing different companies' profitability.

- EBITDA isn't shown in the financial statement, but you can, and should, work it out yourself. Take the EBIT figure, and add back the depreciation and amortization. What you're looking at here is basically the cash operating profits.

- Finance is the next item in the accounts - interest paid on any debt, interest received on any cash, and other finance charges or gains and losses on investments.

- Pretax profit (or loss) is EBIT less finance. This shows what the business makes before it pays corporate taxes. It depends both on the intrinsic profitability of the business, and on the way that it's financed; a company that makes a profit on its operations could still make a pre-tax loss if it has taken on too much, or too expensive, borrowings.

- And next up: tax. Note that tax isn't calculated by the tax authorities on the figure that's shown in the P&L, because the tax authorities have different ideas about what is an allowable expense from the auditor, and also because a company may have all kinds of special tax breaks, foreign subsidiaries paying different tax rates, or R&D tax credits. So although the tax figure will normally hover around the base level of corporate tax, it could be higher or lower to reflect those adjustments.

- After tax we have our net profit (or loss), but there's one more item to take out: minority interests ("income attributable to non-controlling interests"), where the company has to pay out to minority shareholders in one of its subsidiaries. This is very rarely a significant number.

- Net profit is what the business has available to pay dividends from. Technically, it can pay dividends even if it doesn't make a profit, out of reserves. But this is usually only a temporary measure, taken if the company has one bad year due to a one-off event but expects to return to profit next year. What remains after paying dividends goes to reserves, that is, it adds to the balance sheet total. Net profit is the key measure for understanding a business's returns to shareholders.

We should also talk about "normalized earnings." Often, earnings in a single year can be affected by a big one-off item. Suppose a tornado destroys your factory roof, and you can't manufacture for a month while you're getting repair work done. Suppose a major lawsuit goes the wrong way for you, or you have to trim your branch network and there are some major redundancy costs to be paid. Or suppose you book a huge profit on the sale of your old office site for redevelopment - that would boost your profits this year but next year's figures won't be comparable.

That's why accountants, as well as investors and Wall Street analysts, want to adjust the figures to give an idea of the 'regular' profit for the year. Analysts usually produce 'normalized' figures so they can value the company on its normal profits rather than an outturn figure that might include a number of one-off items.

There are all kinds of detailed accounting arguments involved, but unless you're an auditor, it's very much a matter of your own judgment what you decide is a one-off and what you think is just a regular cost of doing business. For instance, a brewery which sells off a downtown bar that it owns and makes a huge profit might validly say that's a one-off. But a brewery which has a dozen such bars and trades in and out from time to time should probably admit that it's got a side business as a real estate developer.

We've had a good look at the P&L - let's turn the page and look at the balance sheet next.

Chapter 3 – The Balance Sheet

The profit and loss account worked as a big subtraction formula. The balance sheet is all about addition. It's also different in that it has two sides - assets and liabilities. It shows what the business owns, and what it owes - its assets (machines, buildings, inventories, and so on) and its liabilities (borrowings, sums owing to investors or suppliers). That basically tells us how much the business's assets are worth at the balance sheet date- though it won't tell us how much money it can make with them. While the P&L shows flows of money in time, the balance sheet freezes the company on a single date.

To explain assets and liabilities - and the idea of the 'balance' - we need to go back to the very origins of accountancy, when bankers like the Medici in Renaissance Italy were starting to draw up their books in 'double entry' accounting.

According to double entry accounting, every entry you make in a book of accounts needs an offsetting and equal entry somewhere else. For instance, I borrow $30 from James. I put an entry in my debit side, the side that shows 'negative money', money that I owe to people, because I owe him the $30. I also put an entry in my credit side, the side that shows what I own, because I've now got $30 in dollar bills. That means the two sides balance out - and that's where the term "balance sheet" comes from.

Double entry bookkeeping gets a lot more complex than that (some transactions can involve up to 40 different entries), but you get the idea.

The balance sheet has two sides, debit and credit in bookkeeping parlance, but assets and liabilities as far as financial statements are concerned.

- Assets are what the business owns. They might include land, buildings, machinery, software, or copyrights. They might also include money that customers owe and haven't paid (because the business is entitled to it, which is the same as owning it).

- Liabilities are what the business owes. So that could include long-term bank debt, overdrafts, and amounts owed to suppliers. Now, remember that one of the basic principles was that of the accounting entity as distinct from its owners? The business's liabilities also include what it owes to its owners, the shareholders. When investors subscribe to shares, they pay money to the company in exchange for shares of a given face value, and their shares are shown together with the money that 'belongs' to them. This means any profits that have been retained rather than paid out in dividends.

Let's go down the balance sheet and look at the different headings. We'll start on the asset side. Assets are broadly divided into two types, long-term and short-term, or 'current' assets. Short-term, in this case, means under a year.

Under current assets, we see cash and cash equivalents - the latter includes certificates of deposit, short-term bonds, and other investments with which companies try to make a higher return on their cash balances.

Next comes accounts receivable - amounts that are owed by customers. This may be very low in the case of a retailer selling mainly for cash, or very high in the case of businesses that work on the basis of long-term contracts, billing only when project milestones have been achieved (for instance, in the construction sector). You may also see prepaid expenses - this is where rent and insurance that have been paid for future months will be 'parked', for instance, because under the accruals concept they can't be treated as expenses.

Inventories are another current asset. This heading includes not just inventory for resale - for instance, the stock in a retail outlet - but also inventories of raw materials and components, and work in progress. For instance, an upholstery business might have significant money tied up in stocks of fabric and stuffing, but it might also have a nicely finished sofa sitting in the shop (for resale) and a number of chairs at various stages of completion (work in progress).

While normally you'd only look at the overall inventory figure, in some businesses it may be interesting to look at the detailed splits. For instance, if a manufacturing business is running very low on work in progress but has far more than the usual amount of raw materials stocked, what's the reason? Did it have a single, large order that's just gone out? Or has there been a slowdown or outage in production? You'll need to look at some of the other numbers (such as sales), and perhaps do some extra research, to find out.

Now let's look at the long-term assets. These can be tangible or intangible:

- Tangible assets are things you can touch - physical goods, a factory, a shop, machines, cars and trucks, tools.

- Intangible assets can be such things as copyrights, patents, software, goodwill (technically defined - the excess of purchase price over net assets of a company that has been acquired).

Long-term assets, remember, are shown at *historic cost*, since that's one of the basic accounting principles. That may mean the assets are considerably undervalued. For instance, a company that bought its premises twenty years ago may have seen the local area become more desirable, and property prices could have multiplied several times since, while the building will still be in the books at whatever was originally paid for it (plus any refurbishment or addition since them). The principle of conservatism, though, should mean that assets whose real value has fallen are never valued at *more* than they are worth today.

Remember, too, that long-term assets are depreciated depending on management's estimate of their useful life. There's more about that topic further on in the book.

Intangible assets will usually only be shown if they have been purchased, or if their value is certain (as in the case of internally created proprietary software - the cost is that of the man-hours involved in creating it). Business goodwill or brands that have been built up within the business are not included in the balance sheet at all, as it's not possible to give them a specific monetary value. That leads to the rather inconsistent position of showing purchased goodwill, but not organically created goodwill.

So that's the asset side of the sheet; now let's look at the liabilities. Again, these are reported in two main sections: long-term and short-term.

Short-term liabilities will include any overdraft or other debt that's repayable on demand or in less than a year. But there are a number of other short-term liabilities that you need to understand - this is, in some ways, the most complex corner of the balance sheet.

- Provisions are set aside when the business can see a future requirement for spending, but doesn't know exactly how much will be required - a cost that is probable, but not certain. So that could be severance costs, guarantees provided that might be called on, or pension liabilities.

- Payables - sums owed to suppliers from whom the company has bought stocks or services.

- Tax liabilities that haven't yet been paid, but are known.

- Deferred income represents money that customers have paid for goods or services which haven't yet been provided. The business owes the customers something - and until it has provided that service, the money sits in the balance sheet. It's not recognized as revenue till the company has performed its part of the bargain. Again, the accruals basis dictates the accounting treatment of this item.

Long-term liabilities include long-term debt, and that's usually by far the largest item shown. There are a number of other types of long-term liability - sums that will have to be paid out over the long term. These might include the following:

- Capital leases that need to be paid out

- Pension liabilities

- Deferred compensation

- Warranty liabilities

It's worth going through the notes to the accounts to dig out what any major liabilities represent. You might see a large provision for discontinued operations - was that closing down an old business which everyone had expected would eventually have to go, or a new product line which everyone expected to become a huge source of new profits, but didn't work out? Your attitude to the company will depend on what you find out about what those numbers actually represent! Sometimes, too, you might look at the reason for the provisions and think the company has underestimated the funds it may need to pay out - for instance in the case of a major product recall.

There's one other area of the liabilities side of the balance sheet, and that is shareholders' funds (or shareholders' equity). This represents what the business 'owes' its shareholders: the money they subscribed for shares, and the retained profits of the business. The aim of the business should be to grow this every year - and to grow it through retained profits - not by just issuing more shares. If it issues more shares, sure it's getting funds in return, but it will have to divide its earnings between more shareholders. On the other hand, if it increases profits, every existing shareholder will have a share in that increased, retained profit figure.

One important thing about the balance sheet is that it gives you a total valuation of the assets used in the business. You can calculate book value per share - the part of the total value of the business that each share entitles a shareholder to. Now, remember that this is a historic value, and it's only the value of assets, cash, receivables, and so on. It's not the value of the business as a profit-generating enterprise, which might be considerably more. But it's a good figure to know. It's pretty much the absolute bottom dollar anyone would pay for a business (unless there are huge liabilities, like lawsuits against asbestos producers, for instance).

Contrarian and value investors often look at businesses where the share price is below the book value per share as potential investments. There may, of course, be a good reason for the discount - the book value might not reflect events that have happened in the current financial year, and which will greatly reduce the value of the assets, or there may be fraud going on.But otherwise, being able to buy a stock in an out-of-favour industry for less than asset value vastly reduces the risk of a purchase and suggests the stock is being bought at a price that gives room for very significant capital appreciation.

Net book value per share is also an important figure for investment trusts, real estate investment companies, and other asset-rich companies. Sure, you may be buying a REIT for the stream of recurring income you expect over the years, but knowing how many dollars of real estate assets you get for each dollar of your money you invest is useful as a short cut valuation.

Chapter 4 – Sources and Uses of Funds

We've talked quite a lot about the accrual basis and the fact that the profit and loss account doesn't reflect actual cash movements, which can be quite different. That's why businesses are also required to show a cash flow statement which shows the actual flow of funds. It's incredibly important to both business managers and investors, for various reasons:

- It captures working capital flows, which can put a financial strain on fast-growing businesses or ones which grant extended credit to customers, or need to maintain high inventories.

- It shows investment in fixed assets and lets you see whether the business is 'buying' profits with cash outflows. You can't see these investments so clearly elsewhere - if you look in the balance sheet, you only see the sum total of assets, and though you could work out the year to year change, the total will be affected by depreciation as well as by new investment.

- The cash flow account is often where you can spot the effect of a company trying to improve its profits with creative accounting. It's easy to dress up the profit figures - but it's not so easy to make the cash flow account look good, so this is where you can tell the righteous from the rest.

- You'll also get a good idea of how the company is funding itself - whether it's issuing shares, committing itself to long-term debt, or letting the overdraft take the strain.

- As far as forecasting goes, you'll get a good feeling from the cash flow account of whether the company is coasting, or whether it will need to raise fresh funds to finance its growth - or even to stay in business.

The cash flow account is shown as a series of adjustments to the net income figure you've already seen on the P&L. So the net income goes at the top. Next, we look at the operating activities of the company and what finance they sucked up, or what cash they contributed.

A big element here is adding back depreciation and amortization to the net income - that, remember, was a non-cash cost taken out of revenue in the P&L, so we add it back in the cash flow statement. There will also be adjustments for any provisions or valuation write-downs - again they're not cash, so they're added back. And there will be some adjustments on financial income, but they are usually not large. Tax will be adjusted, because the tax in the P&L is usually tax that will be paid next year, just as the tax paid last year was shown in the P&L last year (and was stored as a provision on the balance sheet). If this doesn't sound clear, don't worry - it *is* confusing till you get used to it.

Next, and very important, is a series of adjustments for working capital. When you have inventory and when you extend credit to customers, you have to finance it. If you keep a continuous level of inventory, you're not using up any more funds than you did already; but if you increase the level of stocks, you're using more cash, so that would be reflected in the cash flow statement by a negative adjustment. The same is true for receivables. So while the balance sheet shows you the actual level of inventories and receivables, the cash flow account shows how much more the company needed to invest in them this year than last (or how much it managed to tighten up its working capital, of course).

The figures are also adjusted for trade payables, and this is where an increase in credit gained from suppliers can help to give a company better cash flow. However, it's wise to be wary of very large increases in cash flow from this source - companies which squeeze their suppliers too hard sometimes end up with problems, and even worse, not paying suppliers could mean the company knows it's in trouble and isn't actually able to pay those bills as they come due.

We've come to 'cash provided by operating activities', that is, the cash flow the business would normally make from day to day. This is a really crucial number. If this is regularly negative, the company won't stay in business long. If there's regularly a good chunk of cash coming into the business, it's healthy. This is the cash that the business can use to pay shareholders dividends, to invest for the future, to acquire competitors or to rebuild a too highly indebted balance sheet. It is, so to speak, the lifeblood of the business.

The next section of the cash flow account is entitled 'cash flow from investing activities', and this is where you'll see acquisitions, disposals, and purchases of long-term assets. Remember, when you spend cash on a new long-term asset, you only show a fraction of that cost in the P&L each year; it's the cash flow account that will show the whole amount.

Usually the big item is investment in long-term assets. Those might be tangible (production facilities, vehicles, new retail outlets, tools) or intangible (copyrights, for instance when a publisher buys another publisher's back catalog; software). Generally, you'd expect there to be a fairly regular trend, except in very capital-intensive industries like mining or chemicals, where you might see big swings in capital expenditure (capex for short). It could be a major project for three years, and then relatively minor for some time after that. If there's a major change in the number, you'd want to look at the management discussion to see why that is. It might be a timing difference (a project delivered late, perhaps) or it might mean the business has changed its strategy.

Acquisitions of other companies will be separately noted. There will also be lines for disposal of long-term assets. For instance, a sale of fleet vehicles when they get to a certain age, or sale of properties that are surplus to requirements - and disposal of businesses. Depending on the company, there may also be lines relating to the acquisition or disposal of securities: long-term bonds held for income generation, or shares held in other companies.

The figure of operating cash flow less cash flow from investing activities is a particularly interesting figure for the investor. Oddly, it's not actually shown in the statement - so you will need to work it out for yourself. This figure can sometimes show that though a business appears to generate chunky cash flow, in fact it needs quite a high level of investment to do so. That might make it a bit less attractive to a buyer and increases the level of risk of its activities. To get a really good feeling for the business you're going to want to look at this figure over several years to see how it varies from year to year, and get a feeling for what it is normally (or for the cyclicality of the business).

Finally, the cash flow shows cash from financing activities. There are two main areas of concern here. One is dividends paid to shareholders. This shows the dividends actually paid in the year, whereas the P&L shows the dividends relating to this year's profits. Some of those may have been paid, like quarterly and interim dividends, but the final dividend won't actually be paid till next year). Again, the accruals basis means that the P&L and the cash flow statement show different aspects of the same transactions.

The other area of concern in this part of the statement is financing through the issue of shares or debt. If the company has issued shares, the money it has raised will be shown in the cash flow - it won't be shown in the profit and loss account. The cash flow will also show the raising of debt, and any debt repayments. There may be more complex items; for instance, a retailer might raise funds by selling the freehold of sites that it owns, and entering into a contract with the purchaser to rent the premises - a *sale and leaseback* of this type will be shown in the cash flow statement.

All of the different financial statements are linked to each other, and the cash flow is no exception. The figure for cash flow after financing, at the bottom of the cash flow statement, should be the same as the figure you get if you calculate the change in net cash from the balance sheet.

Some analysts like to calculate another figure: cash flow before debt raising. Simply take the cash flow after investing activities, and adjust only for equity raising and dividends. That gives you a feeling for the basic business cash generation of the business plus the raising of stable equity finance.

With the cash flow statement, always look at trends over time. Annual reports show two years of financial statements, but that's not nearly enough to do a proper analysis. We'd generally prefer to get five years, but at least three, to get a feeling for the broad trends, and that's particularly true when it comes to the cash flow account. Simply looking at the overall operating cash flow and investing cash flow should give you a good idea what kind of company you're dealing with. Does it generate cash every year or does it leak cash? This is the case with some growth companies but also with failing companies, so you'll need to do more research to work out which of the two you're looking at. Maybe the company has some cash generative years and some in which it spends cash? You'll also want to get a good feeling for the capital expenditure items. Again, different companies have different profiles when it comes to capex, and you may find a more detailed breakdown of what the money is spent on in the discussion of operations or the notes to the accounts.

Chapter 5 – Notes to the Accounts

So far, we've looked at the main accounts in the financial statements. However, every analyst knows that the real action is often not shown there, but in the *notes to the accounts*. Some of these notes are actually completely useless to you, while others hide nuggets of pure accounting gold - but you're going to have to read it all to find out which is which. It's an incredibly painstaking and sometimes quite boring thing to do - until you hit paydirt, and then it can become really interesting. You'll need to call on your internal geek or nerd to succeed!

In this chapter, we're going to start referring to two sets of accounts, from US retailer, Sears, and European airplane manufacturer, Airbus, so you can see how things work in real life and what we might find out about a company by looking at the notes to the accounts. We'll be going into more detail about analyzing these companies later on, but for the moment we're just going to concentrate on how to make your way through the notes, what they mean, and how to use them in your analysis of the company.

Let's start off with the *Basis of Presentation* or *Summary of Significant Accounting Policies*. This simply tells you how the company has chosen to show its results - what accounting policies it has used in presenting the financial statements. You're looking for a number of things here, probably the most important of which is any changes since last year. Companies sometimes have good reasons for changing policies, for instance if the nature of the business has changed, but more often, it's done to make the accounts look better.

Here are some other important things in here that you need to know:

- Revenue recognition. When does the company recognize revenue? If it is engaged in long-term contracts, this can be an important factor. You might also be surprised at what's included in revenue; Airbus points out that revenues includes the aircraft engines, although the customer buys those directly from the engine manufacturer. You can see that Airbus has two types of business - airplanes is a typical manufacturing business, but there's also a contract business which recognizes revenues according to the percentage of the contract that has been completed.

- Provisions. When does the business make provisions for loss-making contracts or bad debts? Sears tells us quite a lot about the provisions made when it closes a store location - and since it's a business that's shrinking rather than growing, that's important to know.

- Research and development. Are costs capitalized or expensed? That is, are R&D costs taken out in the profit and loss account, or are they squirreled away on the balance sheet? Airbus only capitalizes R&D when it has a clearly identified, feasible product and business plan, or when it creates new tools and jigs for the production process. 'Pure' research, therefore, is expensed.

- Inventories. This usually isn't a contentious item but it's worth understanding exactly how inventories are valued. Sears uses the Retail Inventory Method, RIM, to value its stocks. It's widely accepted, but it's based on rather a lot of value judgments on markups, markdowns, and so on. It's intriguing that the treatment is different for Kmart and for Sears Domestic. That probably reflects the fact that Kmart acquired Sears back in 2004, and the two historic accounting policies have never been brought together.)

- Key estimates and judgments. This is a useful section as it will show you what the auditors feel are important matters of judgment that affected the figures. Ninety percent of this section is boilerplate, at a high level of abstraction - but you can also find some interesting insights into the business, and particularly you'll see which areas of the business the auditors found most uncertain or difficult to evaluate. That's useful to know. For instance, Airbus' auditors focus on the commercial and military aircraft programs as involving an increased level of estimates, which introduce uncertainty into the accounts, and point us in particular to the A350 XWB and A400M programs. That shows you exactly where the pain points are for Airbus.

- Scope of consolidation. Most larger companies have subsidiary companies whose accounts are included in those of the parent company. Some may also have special purpose vehicles set up for a particular purpose, such as operating a particular contract or owning a property. This section will tell you what's going into the accounts. It's particularly useful where a company has lots of joint ventures, as it will show you how their profits are accounted for. Look at the Airbus section on joint ventures; it's quite complex, but well explained.

- Acquisitions and disposals. This will show any businesses that have been acquired or disposed of in the period, with details of how they have been accounted for. You'll also find details of any assets that are up for sale.

That's preparatory work for reading the notes. You may have spent half an hour or so and perhaps you don't feel you have got much out of it; look at this as your insurance. You can imagine that you've looked around the house you want to buy, and you've wasted your time - you haven't found any termites, you haven't found any subsidence, and there are no holes in the roof. That's good news!

You also know that if you get confused at any point about where particular items are shown in the notes, you can look back to the Basis of Presentation - the notes are almost always cross-linked and that can be very helpful as an index. You might want to do a bit of flicking through the statements right now to see how all that cross-referencing works.

Some notes are always there: fixed assets will always have an explanatory note showing how the assets are made up, and also show the historic cost and depreciation for each class of assets; there will always be a note on equity. But other notes may only be added if they're needed. For instance, there may be notes on major property transactions, pension fund liabilities, or closures of business. Always spend a few minutes looking through the headings of the notes to see where there are 'special' items.

Segment information

Let's take a look at the *Segment Information*. Almost all businesses other than the smallest and simplest split their operations down several ways. It might be geographically (US, EMEA, Rest of World), by business line (tablets, smartphones, other), by service vs product, by different brands, or in various other ways. You can sometimes tell quite a lot about the way a company's management sees the world by the way it has chosen to report its segment information.

This is shown in note 17 of the Sears accounts, and we get a breakdown of revenues between Sears and Kmart, and between different retail lines - hardlines, apparel and soft furnishings, food and drug, services, and other income. However, there's no breakdown of gross margin by retail line. Airbus divides its activities into commercial aircraft - by far the majority of revenues - helicopters, and defense/space, and splits those activities down as far as the net profit level. It also shows the assets used in each activity - we'll see later how you can calculate the return on assets for each activity, to see whether the company is using its assets in the most effective way.

Fixed assets

There's usually a good-sized section on Property, plants and equipment. In the Airbus report you can see that the biggest item is technical equipment and machinery. You can also see that it depreciates more quickly than real estate holdings. The historic cost has been written off by quite a large amount, though it's still the biggest investment after depreciation. There's also a big construction in progress item. That says Airbus' assets are for the most part specialized assets, and perhaps they wouldn't be easy to resell in a liquidation.

Airbus also tells you about its off-balance-sheet commitments: future lease payments and commitments to buy real estate and other fixed assets.

Sears has a lot of information on real estate transactions, so much that you might wonder whether it's worth looking at the company as a real estate investment rather than a retailer. On page 18 it gives a list of stores by state and by type, though that's not strictly part of the financial statements. The split of fixed assets by type is actually given in the balance sheet - you can see that land, buildings and improvements are by far the majority of assets.

Note 11 in the Sears financial statements shows you the detail of real estate transactions. There are several pages of closely written text and tables. First of all, we see that Sears made a profit on its real estate. It didn't, if you remember, make a profit on its retail sales, so selling off its surplus assets seems to have become the main profit-generating business. There's quite a complex transaction involved here, and you'll probably have to read the note twice to even begin to understand it. The Seritage joint venture can make money by taking over old Sears stores and renting them out to new premium tenants, like Pottery Barn Kids or Williams-Sonoma. It's part-owned by Sears CEO Eddie Lampert, who also owns 58% of Sears. What the financial statements won't tell you, but you can easily look up, is that the stock market values Seritage at nearly one and a half times the value of Sears stock.

You should also look at note 14, which gives details of Sears' lease commitments for future years. These appear to decline quite significantly from the current year onward, which is good news - the company's cost base should be shrinking.

Inventories

Financial statements should show the split of inventories between different stages of stock. Note 20 in the Airbus accounts shows you that by far the biggest category of inventory - as you'd probably expect - is work in progress. But it's interesting to see that there are some pretty big write-downs of inventory, which tells us that Airbus quite often finds its costs on a contract are going to exceed the price it will get. That might be a bit of a concern for investors (or suppliers). Sears doesn't give a breakdown - but then, as a retailer, it only has one kind of inventory, the merchandise in its stores.

This note is worthwhile because you want to know how well a business is converting its inventories back into sales. For instance, if it has a huge stockpile of raw materials, that might be holding back performance (though it might also reflect a management decision to reduce the risk of a price rise or shortage of supply). If you see low raw materials and low work in progress, but very high finished goods stocks, that suggests sales may have slowed - will the business be able to sell its product? Analysing stock movements lets you see right inside the business, if you do it right.

Borrowings

There will always be quite an extensive note on a business's borrowings. This is useful, as it can tell you about any conditions attached to debt (for instance if it is secured on the company's assets), and about the maturities of any borrowings. Maturities can be important; if a large amount of debt is due to be repaid next year, the company either needs to find the cash, or be able to refinance. If it can't do either, life can get very difficult.

Sears note 3 tells you about its borrowings. In the first paragraph you can see that its short-term borrowings have gone from zero to $915m in the last year, while total debt is almost flat. Long-term debt is down, and if you look at the bottom of the table you'll see the rate that Sears is paying on average has gone up from 7.2% to 7.6%, so it hasn't been getting rid of the most expensive debt first. Further down, you can see that $979m becomes repayable in 2018, and almost all the debt needs to be repaid or refinanced within the next three years. That's not very good for a company that's not making a profit. How likely do you think it is that Sears will be able to refinance at a good rate?

Note 34.3 in the Airbus accounts tells you about long-term finance liabilities, and again, you can see the maturities and amounts of each type of debt.

Benefit plans

This is one of the most boring and technical areas of the financial statements - even many analysts admit to finding it difficult. But when a large and old established company is shrinking, pensions liabilities and other employee benefit liabilities can come back to bite it. An example is British Telecom, which took over a pension fund designed for a very large state enterprise. Three decades later, it has substantially fewer staff and operates in a much more competitive environment, but it has liabilities relating to pensioners from a much larger enterprise. This is a very common problem with companies that were state owned utilities but have since been privatised - no fault of the management, who have inherited expensive and sometimes not particularly well funded pension schemes. If you're looking at a formerly state-owned company, always look in great detail at this note to the accounts.

Sears is another company with the same problem. In Note 7 you can see what it's done to try to address the issue; it has transferred liabilities to MetLife, buying annuities for its retirees and thus 'de-risking' the underfunded pension plan. However, it states that "Contributions to our pension plans remain a significant use of our cash on an annual basis." It's always worth looking at these kinds of liabilities, as they're the kind of things that a company can ignore while it's growing - but can make recovery very difficult.

Store closings and severance

Note 13 to Sears' accounts shows how the costs of store closings are divided up between lease terminations, markdowns on inventory, and severance costs. The balance appears to be different at Kmart, with markdowns the biggest item by a long shot, and Sears Domestic where they're a bit less important. The note also shows you how these costs have been treated in terms of the accruals basis - how much was taken this year and how much is still to come.

Another useful thing about this note is that together with the store numbers included in the discussion of operations, it lets you work out an average cost per store closed. That could come in useful if the next Sears trading update mentions further closures to come.

Earnings per share

There's always a note showing the calculation of earnings per share. You already know what net income the company generated, but this note will show you the average number of shares on which EPS was calculated. That's not the same as the number of shares actually in issue, since if shares were issued part way through the year, they only get a pro rata share of earnings for the months in which they were in issue.

You'll also see a figure in many accounts for *diluted earnings*. This takes into account shares that haven't yet been issued, but will be or could be; for instance: under staff compensation schemes, on the exercise of options, or where convertible bonds have been issued and could be converted into shares. You need to check this figure, as sometimes the difference between EPS calculated on existing equity and the diluted EPS is quite significant. Basically, you have the same pizza, but it will have to be shared among those of you around the table and a large number of late-arriving guests.

Diluted EPS comes into its own when a company decides to fund an acquisition through the issue of shares. There will be more profit, because the acquisition's profits will also be accounted for this year - but there will be more shares, too. When a smaller company has been acquired, it's common to give directors of the company - who may also have been significant shareholders - notes entitling them to have shares issued in the future, or options, rather than shares, in order to tie them in for a couple of years. Unless their entitlement to a future share issue is recognised, the current EPS will overstate what's due to other shareholders.

Related party transactions

Nine times out of ten this note isn't very important; it might show that the company has helped one of the directors buy a car, or sometimes with smaller businesses, that a director has put his or her own money into the company.

But note 15 of the Sears accounts is interesting. It shows that the chairman is also the head of ESL, a fund which owns 49% of Sears stock, 67% of Lands End, spun off from Sears, and 58% of SHO, as well as a significant stake in Seritage. All these businesses are interlinked to some extent, and you can track the links through this note. It's worth noting that in 2017 Sears ended up paying $40m to settle a lawsuit by Sears shareholders who asserted the sale and leaseback to Seritage was done at below market prices, though Sears shareholders were entitled to buy shares in Seritage in proportion to their holding in Sears. Related party transactions can be a way to asset-strip a company or take an unfair remuneration out of it, though of course that isn't always the case. Read through this note and make your own mind up!

<u>Employees</u>

This isn't really a financial number, but it's a very important one when you start analyzing a company. How much is each employee paid - has that number increased or declined? For instance, a tech company or consultant might find the market for new hires is competitive, and have to increase what it's paying. How much revenue does the business make for each employee - and how much profit? You'll want to know the answers to those questions. Airbus shows the answer in notes 26-27, and also splits the employees by sector. Sears shows the total number on page 5, but doesn't split it down, or give a comparative figure for the previous year.

By the way, think about which financial statements were easiest to find your way around, and which were most useful - which gave you more understanding of the way the business works? We selected one US statement, and one European report. You might like to reflect on some of the differences. They're both very much driven by regulatory requirements, but have different emphases and formats.)

Bear in mind that you haven't started doing any analysis yet, but you should already have gotten a flavor of the businesses just by looking at the notes to the accounts.

Chapter 6 – Running the Ratios

This chapter will use the same financial statements as material for the exercise of calculating the ratios. It's more fun than doing a totally invented exercise, it will help us when we get to the next chapter and start drawing some conclusions about Airbus and Sears, and it will also help you find your way around the financial statements. So when you start analyzing accounts for yourself, you'll know where to look for your base data. All those pages of numbers and tiny text look frightening when you start, but most analysts and accountants know their way around and flick through the pages with remarkable speed; once you're used to it you'll be plunging straight in to find the number you want, too. It's just a question of getting used to it.

Most of the important ratios relate either to the P&L, or to the balance sheet, or both. When you're measuring the return on assets, or the speed with which stock turns over, you're calculating a ratio that compares profit measures with the balance sheet. There are also a number of ratios you might use that go beyond the purely financial. They may not be shown in the financial statements, but it's worth checking out presentations to investors which often show ratios based on customer numbers, employee figures, or other factors. These might include:

- Revenue to available seat miles (for an airline)
- Revenue per subscriber (telecoms, pay-TV)

- Occupancy and revenue per room (hospitality)

- Bad debt % (banking)

- Utilization rate (services)

- Availability / uptime (system operations in computing companies)

- Starts, completions, average price per dwelling (housebuilding)

Stock market analysts used to use calculators, paper and pencil. That's way back in the old days. Now, most analysts and most serious investors have spreadsheets already set up, into which they can plug the numbers and get the ratios calculated automatically. That's definitely the way you want to go - but for this exercise, while you're learning your way round the financial statements and the ratios, it may be better to do things the old school style. Get out your calculator (okay, we're in the modern world; use the calculator app on your smartphone) and work out the figures one by one. It will really get you thinking about how you are performing the calculation and help the basic principles stick in your mind.

The Profit and Loss Ratios

Profit and loss ratios are really easy to calculate. Almost all of them show a profit level as a percentage of revenues - how much profit does the company make for each dollar of sales?

Gross margin is the most important figure for retailers, representing the mark-up on the goods they sell, so let's look at the Sears report (page 27). To calculate gross margin, we take the gross margin (revenues less cost of sales, buying and occupancy) as a percentage of revenues: GM / revenues * 100. Only you don't need to do it, as the company has helpfully shown the percentage under the relevant lines (still, you could do it just to get used to calculating the figure). It's not such an important number for a manufacturer like Airbus, because the process of converting raw materials and components into the final product adds much more value.

The jury is out on how useful this figure is for services businesses. Some services businesses account for directly billed hours, for instance, as a cost of sales; their gross margin would include hours that an auditor works on an audit for a client, and which are billed to the client, but not hours that the same auditor spends on continuous professional development, marketing, pitching to clients, or speaking at conferences. In that case, you've actually got a useful metric. Other services businesses which bill on a project basis or per job, however long it takes, might report differently.

Operating margin or EBIT margin is an important figure for any company - it's the amount the business makes on trading, before finance and before taxes. It's the basic performance of the business, as a business, reflecting the efficiency of its processes, and its pricing and input costs. Sears makes an operating loss, so let's look at Airbus, instead (page 6). We take 'profit before finance costs and income taxes' as a percentage of revenues.

So for 2016 we get 2258 / 66581 = 3.4%, and for 2017 we get 5.1%. Operating margin has increased quite markedly on sales that were pretty flat. We'll track down some of the reasons for that later, when we do the analysis.

However, because of the accruals basis, operating margin includes depreciation and amortization on purchases of fixed assets that might have been made years ago. We might also be interested in what the margin is before depreciation and amortization - the 'cash profit' being made, so to speak. That's why we'll also calculate a margin for a figure that's not shown in the statements, **EBITDA:** earnings before interest, tax, depreciation and amortization.

We need to go to either the notes to the accounts or the cash flow statement to find the depreciation number. We add that back to the operating profit. This is EBITDA. Then we calculate EBITDA as a percentage of revenue.

The first step then is to go to page 10 and get the depreciation number; it's almost the same for both years. Add this to the operating profit and you should have EBITDA of EUR 4552m for 2016, and EUR 5719m for 2017. Then calculate the percentage, and you should get an EBITDA margin which progresses from 6.8% in 2016 to 8.5% in 2017.

EBITDA margin = (EBIT + depreciation + write-downs) / revenues * 100

Looking at Sears, you can see that for two out of the three years reported, EBITDA was negative. Even when you add back depreciation and the impairment charge (another non-cash item) you don't get a profit. And in 2017, EBITDA was a miserly $44m, or 0.3% of sales.

Pretax margin and **net margin** are very similar, except that they use the post-interest and post-tax income to calculate the ratio. You can work those out on your own. The net margin is a particularly important one for shareholders, as this is the amount that 'belongs' to them once all the other stakeholders - suppliers, banks, and the tax department - have been paid. But remember that both these figures can be profoundly affected by the way a company is financed, so they don't necessarily provide a good handle on how efficiently the business's operations are being run.

There's one more ratio we want to calculate from the P&L before we move on to the balance sheet, which is: **interest cover**. This shows how much wiggle room a company has, financially - how many times over can it pay its interest bill? It's similar to the calculation you might make if you're offered the job of your dreams, but it's at a lower salary than the job you're doing now - how well covered is your mortgage?

To calculate interest cover, we take operating profit, and divide by net interest expense. Now, some people get picky and exclude other finance charges, while others bundle all the financial items together.

Generally, the version you pick isn't going to make a huge difference to what the ratio tells you.

Interest cover = EBIT / (interest expense - interest income)

For Sears, you've got an operating loss, so it has no interest cover at all. For Airbus, for the latest year, you have interest expense of 517, but you need to net off interest income of 189. That gives us a net interest expense of 328. Divide EBIT of 3421 by that, and you get 10.4 times, so Airbus is happily out of the danger zone. Normally, interest cover should be at least 2x for a company to be considered 'safe'. That gives it room for the occasional bad month or quarter without running into problems paying its interest charges.

The balance sheet ratios

Now let's look at the balance sheet. What we're looking at here is mostly the financial structure of the company.

The **gearing,** or debt ratio, measures the amount of debt as a percentage of the company's assets. It's similar to loan to value, which you'll have come across if you have a mortgage - the higher the percentage of your house price that's represented by debt, the more likely you are to get wiped out in a property crash. There are two ratios we can use: debt to equity, which compares what the banks own to what shareholders own, or debt to total assets.

For the Sears balance sheet, we want to get a figure for total borrowings, so we need to add together short-term borrowings, the current portion of long-term debt, and long-term debt and lease obligations. For the 2018 financial year, that's 915+968+2249 = 4132. Subtract cash of 182 to get 3950. Restricted cash usually represents cash that the company can't touch, possibly because it's held in escrow, so we're not going to take that away from debt.)

Sears actually has a deficit of shareholders' funds. That's uncommon and it means the company is really in trouble - like a homeowner who's living in negative equity with the house worth less than the outstanding mortgage. If the company was liquidated at the balance sheet value, shareholders would get nothing. So we can't calculate debt to equity. We can, however, calculate debt to total assets. 3950 / 7262 gives us 54.4%.

debt ratios:

(short-term borrowings + long-term borrowings - cash) / shareholders' funds

(short-term borrowings + long-term borrowings - cash) / total assets

The gearing numbers are important because they illustrate the risk/return profile of the company as an investment. If a company is growing fast, plenty of debt means that once the interest charge has been paid, the rest of the profit is shared out to a relatively small shareholder base. Returns to shareholders will be higher than they would without that debt. Just imagine you buy a house without putting any money down - you'll get every penny of any price increase once you've paid the interest bill. On the other hand, a failing company with high gearing may result in shareholders getting completely wiped out and the banks taking everything to pay off the debt.

If a company is liquidated with no debt, all the funds raised go to the shareholders. That doesn't always mean bankruptcy. Some investment companies, like REITs, are set up for a limited number of years, with the intention of returning cash to shareholders through an orderly liquidation at the end of the period.

Working capital ratios

Working capital ratios look at how well the company is managing its short-term assets and liabilities. Does it turn over stock fast, is it getting paid on time by its customers, and are its suppliers giving it enough credit?

Let's look at Sears again for inventory. Merchandise inventories are shown under current assets, and we compare those not with sales (which are marked up from the stock price, of course) but with the cost of goods sold (COGS). Average inventory divided by COGS is multiplied by 365 (the number of days in the year), so we get 2798 / 11349 * 365 = 90 days.

Inventory / COGS * 365 = days' stock

But we should refine that a bit, because the stock shown in the balance sheet is the inventory at the end of the year. We're more interested in the average inventory during the period, and the best way to estimate that is to take the starting stock and the stock at the end of the year, and average them out. That's 2798 + 3959 = 6757, which we divide by two to get 3378. If we recalculate stock days, we get 108 days.

We can do the same for trade receivables. Now, Sears has practically nothing, because as a retailer it's selling for cash (or checks or credit cards, which pay it the moment the transaction goes through), not on credit. Airbus, on the other hand, is selling to business customers and generally extends credit to those customers, so it won't get paid for a while after it makes a sale. Look under "current assets" to find trade receivables, and use total sales rather than cost of sales for the calculation. Again, you should ideally use the average level of receivables in the year, rather than just the year-end number. This gives you receivables days, or days' sales outstanding (DSOs).

Days' sales outstanding = Trade receivables / sales * 365

You can also calculate payables days by comparing trade current liabilities with the cost of goods. So then you have a ratio for each of the main items of working capital, and over time, you can see how they improve or worsen. Obviously, the longer you have stock sitting in the shop or factory, the less efficient your procedures and the less speedy your cash flow. Like the circulation of the blood in a human body, the circulation of cash or **cash cycle** needs to be healthy or the business will start to sicken.

So let's do the other calculations for Sears. Receivables are very low as Sears doesn't really sell on credit, so we get 343 / 13409 * 365 = 9 days. With payables, let's ignore the second figure, that if you look at the note, applies to Lands End and Seritage, so they're part of related company deals (Seritage is probably a rent liability). We'll just look at the merchandise related payables - 576 / 13175 * 365 = 16 days. Yes, ideally we'd use the average number, but given the low level of the numbers involved, let's keep it simple.

You can actually calculate a ratio for the **cash conversion cycle** overall now that you have your other numbers.

Cash conversion cycle =

days' inventory + days' sales outstanding - days payable outstanding

The fewer days in the cash conversion cycle, the more quickly the business is getting cash back out of the business after using it to buy stocks or extend credit. Some businesses even have a negative cash cycle, because they get paid upfront and pay their suppliers later. This applies to some supermarkets, particularly those with a very high percentage of food and other short-dated goods, for instance.

So what is it for Sears? 108 + 9 - 16 = 101 days. That's quite long for a retailer. If we added in the Lands End /Seritage figure we'd still have payables days of 59 days, so the cash cycle would be 58, which is quite a bit better, though.

There are two other ratios we should look at that help us understand a business's ability to pay its liabilities as they come due. These are the current ratio and the quick ratio. These two ratios are really useful if you're looking at recovery potential - they show what happens in the worst case scenario if suppliers and banks demand their money back. If the current and quick ratios look good, even a highly indebted company has a good chance of coming through. If they don't, take it as a warning. Equally, if everything else looks okay but these two ratios are sticking up as red flags, you need to do a bit more work on the accounts to see why.

The **current ratio** is calculated as current assets / current liabilities. It includes all current liabilities, both debt and trade liabilities. If it's below 1, then the company could have difficulty paying its liabilities. It doesn't have enough current assets to cover liabilities and it might have to sell off fixed assets to meet unexpected bills. However, some retailers with very short cash cycles manage to live with a low current ratio.

Current ratio = current assets / current liabilities

Let's look at Airbus. Current assets are 59794 and current liabilities are 56025, so the current ratio is 1.07. Only just over 1. That could be a cause for concern.

Sears has 3812 current assets and 4915 current liabilities. That gives a current ratio of 0.78. Now our question will have to be whether we think its cash conversion cycle is fast enough to make that viable?

Let's get right down to the acid test: the quick ratio. This assumes that you wouldn't even have time to sell off your stocks if you needed to meet liabilities quickly, so we'll only look at cash and accounts receivable and any marketable securities (which basically means stuff like certificates of deposit and treasuries).

Quick ratio or acid test = cash + receivables + marketable securities / current liabilities

So for Sears, we get cash at 182, receivables at 343, with no marketable securities shown separately. Compared to current liabilities at 4915; the answer is 0.1. Sears only has ten cents in easily accessible cash to pay every dollar of current liabilities. Whoops!

Return ratios

Now let's look at the return ratios. These are focused on telling us whether the company's assets are being used in the most effective way to create profit and generate cash.

If you had a million dollars, you'd want to invest it to get the best income that you could, while trying to avoid the possibility of losing it all. You might not want to put it all into a jatropha plantation or a tech start-up, even though you might double your money, because those are quite risky ventures. But you don't want to leave it all in the bank and get maybe half a percent return. You want to try to get towards returns of 5-6%, and so you'd want to look at the stock market, perhaps at investing in property, or using peer-to-peer lending or crowdfunding to push your returns up. The same is true for companies; they should be getting the best return that they can on their assets, though they might not want to take some risks - for instance, entering 'difficult' export markets where they're not sure of getting their money out, or getting into a new area of business that requires very high investment without certainty of return. A hotel business might not want to put a new hotel (big investment) into a town that doesn't have one - it would probably rather invest in a town where there's a known demand for accommodation.

When you're assessing returns, there are a number of different ratios that calculate different things and that are relevant to different stakeholders, too.

Return on equity is useful to shareholders, because it shows them the return that belongs to them - what they are getting on their invested capital. It's affected by the capital structure of the business as well as by the efficiency of operations. It's calculated as net income / shareholders' funds * 100.

Let's look at the things that affect this figure. It might be reduced if the company doesn't pay shareholders much in the way of a dividend, but hasn't found a good way to invest surplus cash. That could be a good argument for paying a higher dividend. On the other hand, if borrowings have been used to finance the company, return on equity might be increased - where income from the new investments is higher than the interest payments on debt, the difference benefits shareholders. The ratio is also affected by investment trends. It might be reduced if the company has invested in a huge new asset - a new furnace or a new hotel - which will only start to pay back its investment over the medium term.

Return on assets is more useful for looking at the efficiency of the business overall. It's also calculated using net earnings, but compares them to total assets: net income / total assets * 100. This is the prime ratio for capital-intensive industries, because it looks at the return on the actual assets. So in chemicals, extractive industries, or metals, it's a great ratio to compare companies.

Return on Invested Capital looks at the returns to all finance providers, both debt and equity. It therefore excludes interest from the equation and is calculated as EBIT - tax / debt + equity. So this is a measure of how well the company is using all its finance, whereas Return on Equity showed how well the company was creating returns for its shareholders, but didn't consider debt funding in the figure.

These ratios all looked at profit, but another interesting return ratio is **asset turnover**. It looks at how much in sales each dollar of assets can generate. For best results, as you did with inventory days, use the average assets figure for the year rather than the year-end result.

Asset turnover = sales / total assets

The higher the ratio, the better the company is doing. However, you'll need to compare these figures with other companies in the same industry, as different sectors have different styles of turnover. Telecoms companies generally have quite low asset turnover as they have very large amounts of money invested long-term in their networks. Retailers will have higher ratios, and technology firms even higher. You'll also want to look at the trend in a company's asset turnover and other return figures - remember that they may be affected by a single large investment, particularly in capital intensive industries like utilities or semiconductor manufacturing.

Asset turnover can be compared with other, non-financial data. For instance, transportation companies will have data on air traffic movements or cargo loading that can help you understand how well the fleet is being used; data centers will usually publish capacity utilisation ratios that show how much of the available capacity is earning money. Hotels publish both occupancy data and, usually, average room rate for their different brands. While you may not be able to build a model that actually relates all these ratios together (unless, of course, it's your own business), you can at least take a holistic look at how the different ratios relate, and you may get a strong feeling that one ratio in particular is driving the asset turnover in the business that you're looking at.

Remember, when you're calculating these ratios, that not all of them will have much of a story to tell. For some businesses, particular ratios aren't all that important - a business with mainly cash sales won't have much in the way of receivables, for instance. Other times, you'll find that there are two ratios which really have a big impact on a company's performance, and the others don't tend to vary much. Focus on the ratios that are important and that clearly indicate there's something to look at - the ratios that change between one year and the next, those that are way out of kilter with the industry norm, the ones that seem to be displaying a clear trend. You need to calculate all the ratios, but when you're doing the analysis, there will be two or three you should really focus on.

Again it's like being a crime scene investigator. You need to notice everything - the dropped cigarette end, the gas station receipt in the bin, the scuffs on the entrance door, the wine stains on the carpet. Everything needs to be noted, thought about, and recorded. But possibly only one of these things is going to help you find out what happened and who's guilty!

Chapter 7 – Putting it into practice - Sears

Now let's see how we can put some of our knowledge of financial accounts into practice. We're going to look at Sears and we're going to assess it as investors. We might be thinking about buying the whole shooting match to turn it around, if we were a big retailer. Or we might just be thinking about making an investment in a few thousand dollars' worth of shares.

Let's start by doing a little bit of a search on Google to see if we can find some analysts' views. We might look at Motley Fool, which is a good site for finding finance stories that get beyond the numbers - and that are sometimes quite opinionated. Sears, it turns out, has been doing badly for years. There's a story on Business Insider dated 2014 that predicts it "is headed straight for death" and though it hasn't happened yet, the company hasn't turned around, either.

That will inform what we're looking for in the financial statements. We don't necessarily need to calculate every ratio and look at every number, but we need to find the right clues to answer the big questions we have:

- Is the store concept still marketable? We'll want to look at same-store revenue comparisons. If sales per store are picking up, that will show that the brand is beginning to recover, even if the financial numbers as a whole aren't doing so yet.

- Is stock moving? We'll want to look at stock numbers, the inventory days ratio, and also at the gross margins. If gross margins go up, it means the company is getting better pricing, which is another good sign, as customers are finding the stock more appealing.

- Can the company pay its bills? We want to look quite hard at the costs and liabilities and we need to work out whether one bad quarter could push the company into bankruptcy.

If you look on page 25 you'll find the number of stores is given for the last five financial years. You can then calculate the sales per store in $m. It's a mixed record; it jumps rapidly from 14.8 to 18, but then settles to 15.0 and gradually moves upward to 16.6.

That's a 7% growth in revenue per store last year, against a 24% fall in total revenues. That's not really conclusive. And then we note that the company provides a comparable store sales figure which shows that revenues are continuing to fall. Now, the company has a lot more information than we do on when exactly a store closed, and it excludes sales from stores that have either closed or opened in the last two years so that we get a feel for the performance of the core portfolio. And that performance is bad. It doesn't suggest shoppers are headed back to Sears.

At this point, you might want to schedule visits to a few stores. If these numbers are to be believed, you'll see a store with very few customers and not much life. That would confirm the story of the statements. Remember, financial statements are a bit like an ECG output - a doctor can tell quite a few things from it but she's still going to want to take a look at the patient 'in the flesh'. One of the key skills in interpreting financial statements is relating them to the real world and working out what would confirm the picture you're getting from the financial report, and what might suggest things are changing.

Do you remember we explained how audits are put together and what an auditor's day at work might involve? Think like an auditor - how can you find evidence that confirms what you see in the financial statement?

- Look at financial statements from suppliers or customers to get a triangulated view of what's going on.

- Find industry statistics that can be compared with the company's figures.

- Do a straw poll of people you know in the target demographic (or in business) to find out their views of a product or service intended for them - why aren't they using it? (One fund manager who listened to her 17-year-old son on 'why I don't bother with Facebook any more' well before its August 2018 drop. Maybe she was smart, maybe she was just lucky.)

- Go to an industry exhibition or conference and talk to business people about their experience in the sector. You'll find various stories, some divergent - up to you to interpret them as best you can.

- Look up product reviews in magazines or on internet forums. Sometimes you'll find a company's products are getting very bad reviews quite a while before the business starts to suffer - it can be a good lead indicator - so if stocks are building up, and you're finding critical reviews, it might show you what's going on.

- One investor who got out of the housebuilding market shortly before the credit crunch has a whole load of data she uses to evaluate conditions, including the house price / earnings ratio, the number of cranes she can see from Brooklyn Bridge

Park, and the loan to value and interest rates on mortgages being offered by five major banks. She also gets accounts from REITs involved in multifamily properties, and visits individual developments for sale - tracking how many units are sold upfront, and how many are unsold after families have already moved in. She's a great example of how you could develop your own sources of information if you wanted to cover an industry in detail.

Getting back to Sears, the evidence from the stock numbers is equally inconclusive. Using period end stock numbers it looks as if inventory days have fallen very slightly, from 95 to 90, but then gross margins have continued to decline.

And we already saw that the current ratio and quick ratio look poor, and the company doesn't make a profit, so it will have to pay debt service out of its existing funds. That's not good news.

It's also worth noting that the latest results included a $1648m gain on sales of fixed assets. Without that, the company would have been much deeper in the red.

So where have we gotten to? No evidence of an upturn, and lots of risk. That's pretty much what the analyst at Morgan Stanley thought in the middle of 2017 with a prediction that the company would soon hit the skids. It hasn't yet - but will it?

We can go a bit further in order to try to answer that question. So far, we've worked with the numbers that the company gave us in the financial report. But we can also make a few assumptions and try to answer a few questions about the future.

- If we make a rough estimate of next year's fixed costs based on what we know about the company and the number of stores, what level of sales would it take for Sears to break even? Or to make a reasonable profit?

- What level of gross margin would result in a profit on level sales, given that cost base?

This isn't a forecast. We're just asking what would be *needed*. So, for instance, you might work out the cost of the plane, the cost of the hotel, and the cost of eating out for a week in San Francisco to see what funds you'd need to go on holiday; it doesn't mean you've actually got the money, but at least you know the bottom line that's required. You'll need a spreadsheet to do this, and you need to read all the way through the management discussion of operations, noting any forward-looking statements such as plans for further cost cuts, or cost cuts made this year that will reduce costs next year.

Suppose we assumed, for the sake of simplicity, that next year will see selling and administrative costs and depreciation remain the same, with no impairment charges and no more profits on sale of properties. So we'd want a level of sales and gross margin that would cover $5.4m of fixed costs. That means gross profit needs to be $5.4m.

- If gross margin stays the same, revenues need to go up from $13m to $25.8m - almost doubling. That's not going to happen.

- If revenues stay the same, gross margin needs to go up from 21.1% to 40.7%. That again is not going to happen.

So on the assumptions we've made, it looks extremely unlikely that Sears could break even next year. That means it will either have to cut more costs, or make more gains on the sale of properties.

$m	2017 figures	If gross margin is the same	If revenue is the same
Revenue	13409	25890*	13409
Gross profit	2829	5463	5463
Gross margin	21.1%	21.1%	40.7%#
Selling & Admin cost + depreciation	5463	5463	5463
Profit/loss		0	0

* calculated as the required gross profit / 0.211

calculated as the required gross profit / stable sales figure

Of course, one of the things you'd want to do if you went further with this analysis is to compare Sears' figures with other retailers' results. So, for instance, why don't we look at Walmart? Walmart has a stable gross margin of 24% - 30% higher than Sears - and it only holds 42 days' inventory. You could also look at more direct competitors like JC Penney or TK Maxx. You'd want to look at their financial statements, particularly at their margins and their sales experience, but you'd also want to look at the number of stores - are they opening new stores, or closing down old ones? And what are the sales per store? And you'd probably also want to get a couple of annual reports for past years (2015, 2016) so that you could look longer term at the trends in ratios, or you might decide to analyze the quarterly results.

Anyway, having done an admittedly rather rough analysis of Sears, with a few cut corners and guesstimates, do you think it's worth going on to do any more? Or are you feeling sufficiently discouraged to move on to the next chapter and take a look at Airbus instead?

Chapter 8 – Putting it into practice: Airbus

Airbus had big problems with the A400M military aircraft program. It was subject to delays and was likely to lose money. On the other hand, the commercial business was doing well, with big orders from major airlines like Emirates. Which of the businesses would drive future results? What should investors do? This was the dilemma facing investors in 2017 - working out what kind of animal Airbus was, a growth company with one dodgy business, or a big money pit that was dragging down the profitable side. That's not by any means an unusual question in the investment world, as plenty of companies have two or three diverse businesses with very different performance. (Local newspapers with digital operations turned out, mainly, to be old, poorly performing businesses that dragged down the bright new digital side. You couldn't necessarily have predicted that just from the financial statements, but the figures did give a good steer that might have helped you avoid the worst investments.)

Obviously the financial figures aren't going to give you all the answers. You'll need to make a value judgment on the management and their strategy. You might want to think about the cyclicality of the aviation markets and where we are in that cycle right now. There is quite a lot of non-finance data that could affect your choice.

But the financial figures *will* help you decide whether Airbus has protected itself against the downside, and whether it has enough financial resources to tackle future growth. And they may also help you get a feel for how successful the company has been up to now.

The profit and loss account shows gross profit well up and net income nearly three times what it was a year before. Let's check out what happened to the cash flow account.

Depreciation is pretty much the same as the previous year. But there's a big valuation adjustment to take off cash flow - it's a big swing item, EUR 1,755m. That's a big factor in making cash flow from operations, before working capital, look really quite poor. On the other hand, working capital has been very well managed, with inventories growing by less than they did the year before, and trade receivables actually reducing, thus contributing cash to the business. After working capital movements, the business provided just 1.7% more cash than the year before - EUR 4,444m against EUR 4,369m.

That is a bit of a warning that we shouldn't get overexcited about the profit figures. Then looking at the cash from investing activities, you can see there's a big investment in securities, which ends up vastly increasing the business's negative cash flow from investing.

Let's take a look at the business splits given on page 27. The segment information includes revenue, profit, depreciation and assets, too, so we can work out what each business is making on the assets employed, as well as profit margins.

Profit margins show that every business improved its margins in 2017. Defense actually turned around from making a loss to making a small profit at the operating level. But margins are low; operating margins are in single figures and even EBITDA margins only just break the 10% barrier.

We don't have a net profit split so we'll have to work out return on assets using either EBIT or EBITDA. It might be useful to choose EBITDA so that we can compare more easily with other companies, which might have very different depreciation policies. The commercial aircraft business is not only the most profitable business in terms of profit margins, but it is vastly the best generator of returns, with EBITDA/assets of over 8%, compared to 6% in helicopters and just 4% in defense. Again, considering this is

EBITDA to assets, not net income to assets, that's a bit disappointing - many equity investors consider 8% *net* return a year is about average. Still, this does underscore for us that it's the commercial aircraft business which is the real profit (and hopefully cash) generator in the business.

You'll notice there's also a note showing the geographical dispersion of revenues by customer, since Airbus, unlike Sears, is a global business. What happened in Latin America? Probably the numbers just reflect one big fleet order for a major airline in 2016 that didn't see a follow-up in 2017, but it might be worth digging through the management review of operations - both this year's and last year's - to see what's going on. This note also of course, gives you a rough idea of the currencies that might be important to Airbus. Bear in mind it's domiciled in the Eurozone so if the Euro moves against the dollar, there will be an impact. Something to note for the future.

Note 20 on inventories is quite interesting, because it shows one area of concern: write-downs on stock. Work in progress has been written down by over EUR 6 bn, representing 22% of the gross value of WIP in 2017. That write-down hasn't grown much in 2017, but it's still a worrying percentage of value. As the note says, Airbus writes down WIP when it becomes likely that costs will exceed revenues - that is, that it will make a loss on the project. Obviously, cost accounting and accurate estimation haven't been Airbus' strong suit. If I was talking to management I'd want to know what exactly the reason was behind that write-down, and what measures have been put in place to prevent a recurrence.

It's also worthwhile taking a look at note 36. Airbus is really on the firing line, with several investigations ongoing. There are no figures given for potential settlements; it's too early in the process for any sizable fines to have been leveled apparently - but these various actions could be something of a concern for investors.

We've taken a fast gallop through the Airbus results and we certainly haven't gone into depth on matters like the pension schemes (there's a massive amount of detail in the accounts) or the valuation of financial assets. But it is beginning to look as if Airbus has a reasonably good commercial aircraft business, but a few big weaknesses. It could make an interesting investment, but only if the shares were at a good price. You'd want to ensure that your in-price gave you a good margin of error - right now, the shares seem to be trading quite highly, so that looks like a 'no' as far as buying the shares is concerned.

And of course, what we haven't done is to look at the elephant in the room - Airbus' biggest competitor, Boeing. Boeing always used to be the number one in the industry, and still is, but Airbus has gradually been closing the gap in many areas: it has newer designs, the seats in Airbus planes are wider, and the fuel efficiency is getting better. Meanwhile Boeing's 737 is a very old design; Boeing keeps updating it, but it's probably time they spent some money on an entirely new design that can compete better in the 21st century.

On the other hand, Boeing has a model for every segment of the market, while Airbus has a gap in its lineup - the 200-250 seat airplane. The 777 has that little space all to itself. (Here again, you can see that you need to get to grips with the real business, not just the numbers. You'll only make good investment decisions about Airbus if you understand the market for commercial aircraft. You don't need to *be* an expert, but you need to be able to *find* the experts and understand in detail what they're talking about.)

So let's look at Boeing's financials, grabbing some data quickly from the company's website. Boeing's operating profit margin is 11% - well above Airbus' 6.8% in the commercial aircraft sector - and its EBITDA margin is 13.2%. That says Boeing is doing something right. Its EBITDA margin on assets is 13.4%, again well above Airbus' 8.4%. Airbus definitely comes second when it comes to profitability.

Now there's an interesting point here, which was picked up recently by one market analyst. Airbus has been really good at making sure its order books are full. It has eight or nine years of orders already in the bank, and it managed to pull in another load of orders just before the end of the financial year. But has it been winning orders by cutting prices? Has it been trying to undercut Boeing rather than just trying to make better aircraft or compete in a different segment - for instance with its A380 super-jumbo?

It that's the case, particularly given those WIP write-downs and the problems with a couple of the company's projects, then maybe we should be looking hard at the cost items, to see how efficiently those sales over the next few years will come through to profit. We might even have to track gross margin a bit more actively than we used to. Thin margins, if they don't improve, could suggest recent boosts to the order book have come at the expense of profitability.

Chapter 9 – Depreciation and Amortization – a closer look

We promised that we'd take a closer look at the concept of depreciation and amortization. It's worth doing, as this concept is a bit tricky to get your head around, but once you have, you'll understand financial statements so much better. If you do understand depreciation, by the way, please don't feel patronized or offended that we've included the chapter - it's a bit like riding a bicycle or playing jazz; some people get the idea right away but other people have to look at it quite a while before they get that light-bulb moment. And unless you've worked in finance or had to produce financial statements, it's unlikely that you'll really have an in-depth understanding of depreciation - it's just not the kind of thing that most managers care about or that's included in most management training.

Remember that the accruals concept tries to match revenues to the relevant costs, or costs to the relevant time period. Let's take a really simple business - I'm going to buy a truck and run a delivery service. So the accruals concept says I have to think about how long that truck is going to last, and I have to apportion the cost of the truck over the length of time that I use it.

There are a few ways to do this:

- I can say the truck will last me five years till it's too beaten up to be worth anything, and I can write down the cost by

20% every year till it reaches zero. This is straight-line depreciation.

- I could, theoretically, say that I'm going to do an average of 30 deliveries a week, which over that five-year life is 7,800 deliveries. Then I could write down the cost by a 7,800th for every delivery that I do. This is the activity method of depreciation.

- Some methods also depreciate assets much faster in the early part of their lives. This is useful for assets that could become obsolescent and therefore might be replaced before they are fully depreciated, like computers. The Double Declining Balance method applies double the expected percentage, so in this case, I write the truck down by 40%, instead of 20% (two-fifths instead of one-fifth for a five-year life). Then I take the remaining balance each year and depreciate that by 20%. The depreciation is very steep to start with, but then tails off by the end of the period.

The table below shows how each style of depreciation would deliver - obviously there are some assumptions about how many journeys are being made each year.

	Year 1	2	3	4	5
Truck is bought for	10,000				
Straight-line depreciation	2,000	2,000	2,000	2,000	2,000
Value of truck	8,000	6,000	4,000	2,000	0
Activity method	2,300	1,800	2,000	1,900	2,000
Value of truck	7,700	5,900	3,900	2,000	0
Double Declining Balance	4,000	2,400	1,440	864	518
Value of truck	6,000	3,600	2,160	1,296	778

But a five-year-old truck probably would still be worth something. So most depreciation policies include an assumption about the *residual value* of the assets as well as their useful life. Anyone who runs a fleet of vehicles will probably use one of the price guides that show, for instance, the average value of secondhand cars. So you are aiming only to depreciate the car down to that value. For instance, if you always sell your fleet cars after three years of use, then you will depreciate them over three years to the value you expect to get for them when you sell.

Depreciation links all the financial statements and it's worth following the item between them.

- Depreciation is subtracted from the carrying value of the item on the balance sheet. You'll be able to see a breakdown of the value of assets between their historical cost and the amount of depreciation that's been charged, and that gives you a feel for whether the asset base is relatively new (and not depreciated a lot), or old and tired (and significantly written down from its historic cost).

- Depreciation for the year is also subtracted from the profit and loss account.

- Depreciation is added back to profits in the cash flow account.

You should also look at the relevant policies on depreciation, particularly when you're comparing different companies. For instance, if one company writes off new IT equipment in three years, but another in five, the first company will have lower profits than the second - all things being equal - but the cash flow will be exactly the same. You might also think that some depreciation policies are a little unrealistic. Will a fleet car really last ten years? Or will shop fittings last five?

This discussion of depreciation may seem a bit besides the point, but actually it can be quite a major factor in determining earnings. One telecom company carried out a big project looking at the depreciation of customer premises equipment - that's things like switches installed on a customer's site but which are rented from the telecom company, not owned by the customer. Just by changing the depreciation rate, it could move its costs by one percent - which is quite a step when your margins are not all that high.

Chapter 10 – A Few Tips for the Business Owner or Manager

We've concentrated on analyzing a couple of big companies, for several reasons. First, their financial accounts are easily available. Secondly, they show pretty much everything you'll ever get thrown at you in the way of an annual report. And thirdly, there's a lot of news and analysis on these companies which gives us the chance to link the numbers in the reports with 'real world' trends.

If you want to do a bit more practise, just download the report of any company you think might be interesting from the web, and take a look. You'll probably find yourself puzzling out some differences in accounting - and when you do so, you should also think whether those differences stem from a different business model. For instance, neither of the companies we've looked at are involved in extractive industry (oil and gas, mining) or in real estate investment (okay, Sears has a bit of exposure, but it's not the primary business), and both are involved in the creation or distribution of physical goods rather than in services or software. If you were to look at Amazon, Microsoft, Royal Dutch Shell or Rio Tinto Group, you'd find accounts that look pretty different - because the businesses are very different.

That's the big company world. But the same kind of analysis we've just done on those companies is equally useful for analyzing the operations of a smaller business. Here are just a few things that you might think about.

- Regular financial statements are the best way of catching 'fiddles' such as stock shrinkage, staff taking backhanders, and so on. If your numbers suddenly look very different, for instance if the gross margin on drinks in a bar suddenly falls, or stock numbers don't add up, you know something is going on.

- Once you've worked out your business' return on equity or return on capital invested, you know what a new investment needs to earn in order for it to make sense. Why bother investing in a new area of business if it's not as profitable as what you already have? Of course, if it's very fast growing, you might still want to invest in it. But be aware that you'll be diluting your returns.

- Forecasting your working capital accurately and making sure you have enough funds in place is a massive help to any growing business. It's never comfortable to have to go to the bank asking for emergency funds - and besides, emergency funds always cost more than loans that have been secured ahead of time. Understanding the impact of working capital on cash flow is one of the lessons you've learned in this book that can have the greatest benefit for your business.

- Tracking inventory days and days' sales outstanding gives you advance warning if your business is slowing down or if customers are becoming bad payers. Sometimes, spreading DSOs is the first sign of an industry slowdown - bank credit analysts will tell you that when the going gets tough, payment times get longer and longer. If you're ahead of the game, you can tighten up your stock requirements and your credit policies before things get really bad.

- Checking your margins will give you a clear indication whether your pricing policies are working and whether you are managing your costs well. If you have salespeople who get overenthusiastic about giving discounts to secure new sales, you may see the profitability of your business declining Instead of giving them sales targets, why not incentivize them by seeing how much gross margin they can bring in?

- By looking at your different business activities in terms of their return on assets as well as their profitability or just revenue size, you may find that your return is not coming from the business you always thought was the main generator of income. Analyzing your financial statements in detail can help you focus your funds where they will generate the best return.

You may want to expand your business, at some future date, by buying another business. Your knowledge of financial statements will stand you in good stead then, because you'll be able to read that business's results as an expert, and understand what the numbers are telling you. You'll still need a qualified accountant to back you up, particularly when it comes to going in and looking at the accounting systems, and checking that everything's in order and that, for instance, all sales have been properly recorded and there are no little slush funds hiding somewhere in the business. But you won't have to depend blindly on your accountant, and you'll be able to have a more in-depth conversation about the figures and the business valuation. You'll also know the kind of questions to ask to get to the bottom of what's going on in the accounts.

- No unit information such as sales per branch, or number of billable hours? You're going to want that before you go much further.

- Are inventories much higher than you'd like to see? That's a clue that you ought to take a look at what's in the store cupboard. For instance, does a fashion retailer have a load of outdated clothes? Has a computer shop got a load of old Windows 3.1 machines it can't get rid of?

- Watch like a hawk for any sign of slipping margins. Often, falling margins are the first sign that a product or business is failing - customers are no longer willing to pay as much, and in a couple of years' time perhaps customers won't be willing to pay at all.

- Is the return on assets incredibly low? That might be a sign that the business hasn't been very actively managed; a more ambitious manager would want to get more out of the assets employed.

- Watch out for a business that's growing fast but doesn't seem to generate much cash. That can be a sign of overtrading: inventories are increasing and customers are being given way too much credit to try to increase the sales figures. That kind of business can come down to earth with a real crash.

And of course sometimes, you might start reading the accounts and find in relatively short order that the company has serious problems; it looks as if it's going down the pan, and nothing can save it. Its margins are going down, it's heavily in debt, it can't service its debts and its acid test shows it's dangerously close to insolvency - you now have the skills to calculate and interpret all those ratios, abd yo know what they're telling you. In which case, you can save yourself a lot of time and trouble by forgetting all about it and never bothering your accountant or your bank.

You'll also find that reading the financial statements of companies in your sector can give you an insight into the market that you won't get from anywhere else. It's not at all unusual for the figures to tell the true story while the management discussion of operations remains defiantly - and wrongly - upbeat! But at the same time, it's true that when things pick up, companies sometimes don't like to give hostages to fortune by being openly optimistic - and your first sense that things are looking up might actually come from the P&L.

And the cash flow will often show you things you won't find anywhere else, such as trends in capital spending.

So to recap, as a business manager or owner, you'll get three big benefits from knowing how to read financial statements; first, you'll have a feel for the ratios that help you manage your business properly. Secondly, if you want to acquire another business, you'll have a good knowledge of how to read that business' financial statements and what questions to ask - what items might look suspicious or give rise to pertinent questions. And thirdly, you'll be able to read financial results from major companies in your sector, and get real, actionable business knowledge out of the accounts.

Chapter 11 - Let's think about quality of earnings

Although financial statements are intended primarily to show the quantity of earnings - how much money the business made in any given period - we can also use them to determine the quality of earnings. That is, we can look at how sustainable those earnings are; whether they rely on special factors, whether the growth rate is sustainable (based on strong revenues) or has come from cost cutting (which will eventually come to an end), and whether margins can stay at current levels. If you're thinking about investing in a company's shares, or buying a business, you don't just want to know what it made last year - you want to know that it will continue to make good money in the future.

First of all, you'll want to look at revenue and margin trends over the last few years. As we discussed earlier, you'll want to create a flow of normalised earnings, adjusting the figures in the statements for unusual one-offs. For instance you might make the following adjustments;

- A factory closure in one year made a big dent in earnings. The factory made a product that's not core to the business, and the company has now exited that area of operations completely. You restate profits for that year to what they would have been before the factory closure costs. If you can, you should also take the contribution of that factory out of previous years' results - though that might not be possible if the accounts don't show that level of detail.

- Gross margin is considerably higher than the market standard and you can't find any good reason for this, such as brand power or higher quality product. While you can't really restate the earnings, you might want to do a scenario analysis to see what would happen if the business only made industry average margins - and you'd want to formulate your offer price accordingly.

- The Football World Cup led to a huge rise in sales for a UK based sports bar - particularly since England got further than expected. That might be disclosed in the accounts, or you might want to ask about the level of sales compared to the year before - and then exclude the extra earnings from the figure you're using to calculate the value of the business.

- You might also exclude profits on the sale of a non-core business from the calculation.

Once you've taken out the one-offs, you've arrived at figures which show the normal earning power of the business. But this still doesn't always show how sustainable the earnings are. To get a really good grasp of that, you'll need to check more aspects of the accounts. Run through the accounting policies again to see whether they have been planned to maximise earnings now - that might indicate the profits the company is reporting have been window-dressed in a way that's great for this year and perhaps next year, but maybe not for the longer term.

For instance, a software company that's looking to sell out to a larger firm in the next couple of years might adopt a very aggressive revenue recognition policy. That's great as long as it continues to grow its sales, but it could come unwound if sales start to slow. If in addition it's capitalising a big chunk of R&D, for instance some of the more speculative work it does, then again, it's boosting this year's earnings but if the research doesn't pay off in terms of creating a saleable product, it could come badly unstuck in future.

Depreciation policies are also worth looking at closely. It's easy to boost earnings by selecting a low depreciation rate and a high residual value. But suppose I depreciate my trucks by only 5% a year, and I choose a residual value that's far higher than the real market value of ten-year-old trucks - when I get to the end of the period, my accounts say the pickup is worth $20,000, but the real value is just $7,000. That means I'm going to end up writing off $13,000 if I sell it. Oops. Imagine that variance applied to a major manufacturing plant and you could see very large amounts being written off the value of the company. You'd want to adjust earnings downwards for what you think a more realistic policy would show - or you might want to reconsider buying the business at all.

Look at margins and returns on capital across the industry. They should tally to what you know about the business.

- A business that's top notch, that is well regarded, that is a brand leader or dominant in its sector, can get returns above industry standards. So can a business that's incredibly efficient, that has low input costs, economies of scale from its operations, and efficient distribution. However, if you can't explain high margins or returns in this way, the earnings may not be sustainable - they're either overstated through creative accounting, or have been helped by factors such as a buoyant economy or fashion trend that might not continue. (Bad housebuilders do well in a buoyant housing market but are often found out as soon as the cracks appear.)

- Returns will also often reflect the stage of development of the product, service, or industry. If a product is new and innovative and has just a couple of suppliers, returns can be good - they'll fall once more competitors enter the market. Alternatively, well established, mature industries may have relatively low margins.

- In capital intensive industries, watch out for cyclicality of earnings and returns. That can be difficult to tell from a single company's earnings, but if you look at several companies over the longer term, the main trend will become apparent. Returns can have a lot to do with the timing of investment.

- Apparently high returns on capital can reflect different financing methods such as sale-and-leaseback or the use of special purpose vehicles. There's nothing wrong with these methods per se but you need to be aware that they will change the business model - sale-and-leaseback is great in a stable economy, but can tie a hotel or retail business into rents it can't pay in a downturn.

Check earnings growth against economic growth and against industry averages. A company that's growing much faster than the average needs a good reason - is it growing market share by consolidating its sector or by having a superior product? If not, the figures may be suspect. If it's not growing as fast, then you might want to think about whether the company requires new investment, whether it has outdated product, or whether it's simply been slackly managed. As always, look to link the financial data with 'real world' factors to find out the truth - good analysis of financial statements is very similar to detective work. Think of it as the CSI of business!

You should also check for the type of revenues that a company receives. Are they recurring revenues, like subscriptions or insurance premiums (which are usually renewed), one-offs (like capital investment or big ticket items), or discretionary (purchases of clothing)? One of the great reasons for investing in SaaS (Software as a Service) companies like Salesforce or LogMeIn was that they replaced a computer software model that relied 70-80% on big one-off license sales, with a minority of support services subscription income, with a model that was practically 100% subscription driven. That made their earnings far more sustainable. Clever capital goods companies make sure that they can sell services and consumables alongside their big ticket items, and sometimes report those as a separate product line. That mitigates their dependence on single large contracts.

Watch out for industries that are highly competitive on price. Investors often like to buy the shares of grocery chains "because everybody needs to eat". That ignores the fact of competition. We all need to eat, but we don't all need to shop at Whole Foods. Price wars between grocery chains have often destroyed gross margins in the industry.

Check, too, for dependence on single large customers or large contracts. That introduces a huge risk. For instance, a small jam manufacturer managed to gain a large contract with a major grocery chain. That soon represented 80% of its business. Should it have invested in major new plant and allowed customer credit to build up? Probably not - when the grocery chain decided to take on a new and more trendy jam supplier, the company very nearly folded. Usually, financial statements will show in a note any dependence on single customers, and you'll then need to ask about issues such as the length of the contract, the total receivables due from that customer, and contingency plans should that customer be lost.

Checking the sustainability of revenues is something that most investors realise they should do. However, many miss out on checking out the sustainability of costs, though this is equally important. Companies which buy commodities such as fuel, energy, metals, or foodstuffs, have benefited in recent years from low feedstock prices. Is this going to continue? Will they be able to pass on the cost increase to their customers? But equally, companies using specialist services or products which have only a limited number of sources could be hit hard in the supply chain. That happened a while back when a major semiconductor factory was put out of action - some electronics companies found it very hard to source alternative supply, and ended up with significantly higher costs as a result.

There are several issues here and the financial statements may or may not help you with them. One is cost concentration - whether the business depends on a single supplier for a large part of its inputs. Suppose you could buy two car auction businesses; one buys all its cars from two big fleets, when they come up to the three year mark, but the other one buys from several different corporates and also has a retail purchase program. Which of these has the more sustainable business model?

Worse, a small company in a large industry supply chain could have concentration of both costs and revenues. A high percentage of its components could come from a single supplier and almost all its production might go to a single customer. That's pretty perilous, and it should show up in a note to the accounts.

Finally, check that whatever you see in the profit and loss account actually shows up in cash flow. The real test of profits is whether they increase the business's cash. It's possible that a business which is growing strongly, and which is investing in growth, will show negative cash flow despite having increasing profits - that's the nature of the beast. But if a business that appears relatively mature is not seeing its profits go through to cash, then you should be asking how real those profits are. Track them through - what's preventing the profit from building cash flow? It could be lack of management of working capital, for instance - if the company is granting credit to deadbeat customers, earnings quality is going down even if the base numbers are going up.

Public relations and earnings quality

While PR won't affect the financial figures, looking at a company's PR is a good check on the quality of their financial statements and earnings. If a company is always putting out puff pieces, it might well take a fairly creative approach to its accounts too. There are quite a few things to look out for.

- What is the company's attitude to bad news? Does it usually give investors and customers good, reliable, accurate information - or does it go into denial mode? Look at past annual reports - were problems brushed under the carpet, or does the discussion of operations include a full and frank discussion of these issues?

- Do press releases give real facts and figures, or are they full of jargon ('world class', 'revolutionary', 'disruptive', and so on)? Do press releases about new contracts or developments give figures on the size of the contract?

- Does a single new product or contract get more than one press release? Why? In the worst case, it may reflect delays or relaunches because the pilot project failed - and if those delays or failures have been swept under the carpet, the company's not being terribly honest.

- Read press releases for a full two years and spot the gaps - new launches that are never heard of again, forecasts of huge growth in new markets that are dropped without trace.

Now it's possible that responsibility for this kind of thing comes down to a sleazy PR firm or a single not very ethical employee. But quite often, it indicates that the company is either economical with the truth, or believes its own PR. Make your own enquiries to find out which is which!

Conclusion

We've had a good look around the financial statements and how they work. You should have a feeling for where to start evaluating the information that the financial statements deliver, and we've also given you a few ideas on how you can check in the 'real world' whether the impression that the financial statements are giving you is accurate. We've even given you an idea for how the audit process works - though if you need an audit, call an auditor, don't try to do it yourself!

Hopefully, the Airbus and Sears examples have got you used to looking at real financial statements and finding your way around. You know now that it can be a nightmare and that the useful bits are often hidden in a mass of verbiage. You also know how to calculate ratios and even do a bit of rough forecasting or scenario analysis to test out what the future might hold.

You'll also have a good idea, if you run your own business, of the way different policies can affect your financial figures, and why your auditor is asking all those awkward questions. Just being better prepared for your next audit can save you money - your auditor won't be working as many hours if you've anticipated the data requirements and put together all the right information. And considering what most accountants are paid, even a couple of hours' less work and you've made a decent saving!

Remember that like any skill, reading financial statements needs practice. Look out for interesting business stories on the news, and if they intrigue you, grab the company's annual report and take a look at the raw numbers. Do they bear out what people are saying about the company? Could you have spotted trouble coming in last year's accounts? Do you think the company's fast growth is sustainable? Do you think an IPO is worth investing in? Even if you're not going to invest in the shares, doing this analysis is a great way to get your skills up to speed, and - once you're already a hawk-eyed expert - to keep them honed.

Resources / Sources of information

Not many modern reading lists start off with a book written in 1934. But Graham & Dodd's Security Analysis is the bible. It doesn't matter how long ago it was written, it's still the go-to book for anyone wanting to analyze financial statements. It shows you how to be a great financial gumshoe - trawling the financial statements for clues, detecting financial skulduggery, and hopefully finding some good investments along the way.

If you're intending to apply your knowledge of financial statements to your personal investments, you'll also want to read Benjamin Graham's The Intelligent Investor. And you might enjoy reading some of the annual letters from Warren Buffett and Charlie Munger, on the website of their big fund, Berkshire Hathaway (http://www.berkshirehathaway.com). Not a whole load of financial detail, perhaps, but a lot of good sense about business and investment that you can apply in your own investing.

If you want to go a bit further into financial wickedness of all sorts, Howard Schilit's Financial Shenanigans is a fascinating book. It examines all the ways companies have tried to make their financial statements look better. By the end of the book, you'll appreciate just how much a CFO can do to flatter a company's earnings, but you should also know enough to stop anyone pulling the wool over your eyes.

Accounting Coach (www.accountingcoach.com) provides plenty of information on accounting concepts and regulations, as does the Corporate Finance Institute (corporatefinanceinstitute.com). Investing Answers (www.investinganswers.com) is another good site, with more focus on investors than auditors or bookkeepers as its audience, while you shouldn't underestimate Wikihow (www.wikihow.com) with its clear instructions and neat graphics, for instance, if you want to calculate days in inventory (https://www.wikihow.com/Calculate-Days-in-Inventory).

If you're looking for financial statements, you have a number of places that you can search. Google for the company's own website. There should be an investor relations microsite, and if you're lucky it won't just include annual, interim and (if issued) quarterly statements, but also presentations to analysts and other supplementary information. Or you could head for the relevant Stock Exchange site, whether that's Nasdaq, NYSE or the London Stock Exchange. Company results will be shown on those sites in standardized format, although the London Exchange only shows the results issued on the day, not the full annual report. If you only want outline numbers and not detail, Bloomberg or Google Finance can help out. They'll also give you up-to-date stock prices. And it is always worth checking out what research and news resources your broker or financial advisor offers.

If you want to find industry experts to help link your understanding of financial statements to the business reality behind them, there are several places to look. First of all, trade press interviews can be interesting, though trade press often won't report skulduggery and scandal, or negative views, as it upsets their advertisers. For consumer products look through marketing magazines as well as the sector press - sometimes you ll find interesting information of a more general sort, for instance on demographics or big trends. Also look on accountants' and consultants' websites (Deloitte, PWC, Bain or McKinsey) for sector reviews and news seen from a financial or strategic angle. You might also find individual consultants on LinkedIn - plenty of them have blog posts and other content linked to their personal pages.

Meanwhile, Barron's and the Wall Street Journal have good discussions of industries at top level, though their focus is mainly financial, driven by investors. Because of the financial orientation, trade stories are likely to be reported with the relevant numbers. The investment panel discussions in Barron's are particularly interesting - they're lively, because they're reported from real conversations, and they show how a professional investor or manager arrives at a decision and what kind of data they'll use in doing so.

Appendix: Sears 2017 financial statements

Dollars in millions

	2017	2016	2015
REVENUES			
Merchandise sales	13409	18236	20936
Services and other	3293	3902	4210
Total revenues	16702	22138	25146
COSTS AND EXPENSES			
Cost of sales, buying and occupancy - merchandise sales	11349	15184	16817
Cost of sales, buying and occupancy - services and other	1826	2268	2519
Total cost of sales, buying and occupancy	13175	17452	19336
Selling and administrative	5131	6109	6857
Depreciation and amortization	332	375	422
Impairment charges	142	427	274

Gain on sales of assets	(1648)	(247)	(743)
Total costs and expenses	17132	24116	26146
Operating loss	(430)	(1978)	(1000)
Interest expense	(539)	(404)	(323)
Interest and investment loss	(12)	(26)	(62)
Other income	-	13	-
Loss before income taxes	(981)	(2395)	(1385)
Income tax benefit	598	174	257
Net loss	(383)	(2221)	(1128)
Income attributable to non-controlling interests	-	-	(1)
Net loss attributable to holdings' shareholders	(383)	(2221)	(1129)
Net loss per common share attributable to holdings' shareholders			
Basic loss per share $	(3.57)	(20.78)	(10.59)

Diluted loss per share $	(3.57)	(20.78)	(10.59)
Basic weighted average shares outstanding	107.4	106.9	106.6
Diluted weighted average shares outstanding	107.4	106.9	106.6

Consolidated balance sheets

	Feb 3, 2018	Jan 28, 2017
ASSETS		
Current assets		
Cash and cash equivalents	182	286
Restricted cash	154	-
Accounts receivable	343	466
Merchandise inventories	2798	3959
Prepaid expenses and other current assets	335	285
Total current assets	3812	4996
Property and equipment		
Land	659	770

Buildings and improvements	2432	2954
Furniture, fixtures and equipment	868	1133
Capital leases	151	224
Gross property and equipment	4110	5081
Less accumulated depreciation and amortisation	(2381)	(2841)
Total property and equipment, net	1729	2240
Goodwill	269	269
Trade names and other intangible assets	1168	1521
Other assets	284	336
TOTAL ASSETS	7262	9362
LIABILITIES		
Current liabilities		
Short-term borrowings	915	-
Current portion of long-term debt and capitalized lesase obligations	968	590

Merchandise payables	576	1048
Other current liabilities	1568	1956
Unearned revenues	641	748
Other taxes	247	339
Total current liabilities	4915	4681
Long-term debt and capitalized lease obligations	2249	3573
Pension and postretirement benefits	1619	1750
Deferred gain on sale-leaseback	362	563
Sale-leaseback financing obligation	247	235
Other long-term liabilities	1467	1641
Long-term deferred tax liabilities	126	743
Total liabilities	10985	13186
Commitments and contingencies		
DEFICIT		
Sears Holdings Corporation deficit		
Preferred stock, 20 shares	-	-

authorized; no shares outstanding		
Common stock $0.01 par value; 500 shares authorized; 108 and 107 shares outstanding, respectively.	1	1
Treasury stock - at cost	(5820)	(5891)
Capital in excess of par value	9063	9130
Retained deficit	(5895)	(5512)
Accumulated other comprehensive loss	(1072)	(1552)
Total deficit	(3723)	(3824)
Total liabilities and deficit	7262	9362

Consolidated statements of cash flows

	2017	2016	2015
CASH FLOWS FROM OPERATING ACTIVITIES			
Net loss	(383)	(2221)	(1128)
Adjustments to			

reconcile net loss to net cash used in operating activities			
Deferred tax valuation allowances	(1395)	836	217
Tax benefit resulting from Other Comprehensive Income allocation	-	(71)	-
Depreciation and amortization	332	375	422
Impairment charges	142	427	274
Gain on sales of assets	(1648)	(247)	(743)
Pension and postretirement plan contributions	(312)	(334)	(311)
Pension plan settlements	479	-	-
Mark-to-market adjustment of financial instruments	17	15	66
Amortization of deferred gain on ale-leaseback	(78)	(88)	(52)
Amortization of debt issuance costs and	124	81	60

accretion of debt discount			
Other	(36)	-	-
Change in operating assets and liabilities (net of acquisitions and disposals):			
Deferred income taxes	778	(987)	(519)
Merchandise inventories	1144	1213	(229)
Merchandise payables	(472)	(526)	(47)
Income and other taxes	(108)	80	(95)
Other operating assets	51	(52)	54
Other operating liabilities	(477)	118	(136)
Net cash used in operating activities	(1842)	(1381)	(2167)
CASH FLOWS FROM INVESTING ACTIVITIES			
Proceeds from sale of property and other	1109	386	2370

investments			
Proceeds from Craftsman Sale	572	-	-
Proceeds from sales of receivables	293	-	-
Purchases of property and equipment	(80)	(142)	(211)
Net cash provided by investing activities	1894	244	2519
CASH FLOWS FROM FINANCING ACTIVITIES			
Proceeds from debt issuances	1020	2028	-
Repayments of debt	(1356)	(66)	(1405)
Increase (decrease) in short term borrowings,primarily 90 days or less	271	(797)	583
Proceeds from sale-leaseback financing	106	71	508
Debt issuance costs	(43)	(51)	(50)
Net cash provided by (used in) financing	(2)	1185	(364)

activities			
NET INCREASE (DECREASE) IN CASH, CASH EQUIVALENTS, AND RESTRICTED CASH	50	48	(12)

Airbus SA - financial statements

EUR m

	2017	2016
Revenues	66767	66581
Cost of sales	(59160)	(61317)
Gross margin	7607	5264
Selling expenses	(872)	(997)
Administrative expenses	(1567)	(1726)
Research and development expenses	(2807)	(2970)
Other income	981	2689
Other expenses	(336)	(254)
Share of profit from investments accounted for under the equity method	333	231
Other income from investments	82	21

Profit before finance costs and income taxes	3421	2258
Interest income	189	247
Interest expense	(517)	(522)
Other financial result	1477	(692)
Total financial result	1149	(967)
Income taxes	(1693)	(291)
Profit for the period	2877	1000
Attributable to		
Equity owners of the parent (net income)	2873	995
Non-controlling interests	4	5
Earnings per share		
Basic	3.71	1.29
Diluted	3.70	1.29

Consolidated statements of financial position

	2017	2016
Assets		
Non-current assets		
Intangible assets	11629	12068
Property, plant and equipment	16610	16913

Investment property	3	5
Investments accounted for under the equity method	1678	1608
Other investments and long-term financial assets	4204	3655
Non-current other financial assets	2980	976
Deferred tax assets	3598	7557
Non-current securities	10944	9897
	53941	55037
Current assets		
Inventories	31464	29688
Trade receivables	8358	8101
Current portion of other long-term financial assets	529	522
Current other financial assets	1979	1257
Current other assets	2907	2576
Current tax assets	914	1110
Current securities	1627	1551
Cash and cash equivalents	12016	10143
	59794	54948
Assets and disposal group of assets classified as held for sale	202	1148
Total assets	113937	111133

Equity and liabilities		
Equity attributable to equity owners of the parent		
Capital stock	775	773
Share premium	2826	2745
Retained earnings	7007	4987
Accumulated other comprehensive income	2742	(4845)
Treasury shares	(2)	(3)
	13348	3657
Non-controlling interests	3	(5)
Total equity	13351	3652
Liabilities		
Non-current liabilities		
Non current provisions	10153	10826
Long-term financing liabilities	8984	8791
Non-current other financial liabilities	6948	13313
Non-current other liabilities	17190	16279
Deferred tax liabilities	981	1292
Non-current deferred income	199	288
	44455	50789

Current liabilities		
Current provisions	6575	6143
Short-term financing liabilities	2212	1687
Trade liabilities	13444	12532
Current other financial liabilities	2185	5761
Current other liabilities	29193	27535
Current tax liabilities	1481	1126
Current deferred income	935	917
	56025	55701
Disposal group of liabilities classified as held for sale	106	991
Total liabilities	100586	107481
Total equity and liabilities	113937	111133

IFRS Consolidated statements of cash flows

	2017	2016
Operating activities:		
Profit for the period attributable to equity owners of the parent (net income)	2873	995
Profit for the period attributable to non-	4	5

controlling interests		
Adjustments to reconcile profit for the period to cashprovided by operating activities;		
Interest income	(189)	(247)
Interest expense	517	522
Interest received	149	139
Interest paid	(501)	(378)
Income tax expense	1693	291
Income tax paid	(52)	(559)
Depreciation and amortization	2298	2294
Valuation adjustments	(1755)	1132
Results on disposals of non-current assets	(773)	(1870)
Results of investments accounted for under the equity method	(333)	(231)
Change in current and non-current provisions	805	1321
Contribution to plan assets	(458)	(290)
Change in other operating assets and liabilities:	266	1245

Inventories	(2572)	(3477)
Trade receivables	621	(1215)
Trade liabilities	1419	2398
Advance payments received	1268	4628
Other assets and liabilities and others	(470)	(1089)
Cash provided by operating activities	4444	4369
Investing activities:		
Purchases of intangible assets, property, plant and equipment, investment property	(2558)	(3060)
Proceeds from disposals of intangible assets, property, plant and equipment and Investment property	177	72
Acquisitions of subsidiaries, joint ventures, businesses and non-controlling interests (net of cash)	(23)	(120)
Proceeds from disposals of subsidiaries (net of cash)	377	731
Payments for investments	(913)	(691)

accounted for under the equity method, other investments and other long-term financial assets		
Proceeds from disposals of investments accounted for under the equity method, other investments and other long-term financial assets	532	182
Dividends paid by companies valued at equity	218	192
Disposals of non-current assets and disposal groups classified as assets held for sale and liabilities directly associated	893	1527
Payments for investments in securities	(3767)	(2280)
Proceeds from disposals of securities	2534	2617
Cash (used for) investing activities	(2530)	(830)
Financing activities:		
Increase in financing liabilities	1703	3297
Repayment of financing liabilities	(419)	(1725)

Cash distribution to Airbus SE shareholders	(1043)	(1008)
Dividends paid to non-controlling interests	(3)	(4)
Changes in capital and non-controlling interests	83	60
Share buyback	0	(736)
Cash provided by (used for) financing activities	321	(116)
Effect of foreign exchange rate changes on cash and cash equivalents	(374)	60
Net increase in cash and cash equivalents	1861	3483

Manufactured by Amazon.ca
Bolton, ON

26626866R00061